Sunset Ideas for Storage

By the Editors of Sunset Books
and Sunset Magazine

Lane Publishing Co. • Menlo Park, California

Foreword

Some of the best and most practical storage ideas are
the simplest ones. For that reason, this book emphasizes
variations of basic ideas for you to interpret and expand
as suits you. Some of the solutions are easy to make,
portable, and small in scale. Others are built-in or
structural systems that can be incorporated into a
remodel or a new house.

   An excellent companion to this volume is Sunset's
How to make Bookshelves & Cabinets, which describes
specific construction techniques.

Edited by Maureen Williams Zimmerman

Design and Illustrations: Terrence Meagher

Front Cover: Deep bins built into frame of bed store
               sewing machine, books, bedding (see page 53);
               modular boxes rearrange easily (see page 58).
               Photographed by Norman A. Plate.

Editor, Sunset Books: David E. Clark

Eighth Printing March 1981

Contents

Re-thinking your Storage

Ideally, the knack for organizing possessions efficiently would be inherent in all of us. But apparently it isn't. Crowded kitchen cabinets, overflowing bedroom closets, and tightly packed living room bookcases everywhere show that it's often easier for people to collect possessions than to arrange proper storage for them.

Why is storage important in planning a house or apartment? Basically, storage helps to ease your daily living. It is a means of organizing possessions so that the things you *do* need are at hand and the things you *will* need are put aside, awaiting future use. Perhaps most important, well-planned storage allows you to utilize household space to best advantage.

This chapter will help you define your storage needs, discuss general types of storage units, and explore the ways in which they can be put to use. In later chapters, you'll see how others have solved particular storage problems in various rooms of a house or an apartment in different ways.

DEFINING YOUR STORAGE NEEDS

If you want to find ways to meet your particular storage needs, you'll need to define these needs clearly. Here are a few questions to guide your thinking:

How often is it used?

You reach for the coffeepot each morning, set up a card table on weekends, keep water skis handy during the summer months, and unbox Christmas tree ornaments once a year. How and where articles should be stored depends upon how frequently you use them.

Live storage. Those things you use daily should be stored in the primary living areas of the house—usually as close as possible to where you use them. Don't waste this valuable space on things you use infrequently. Live storage is for articles such as books, records, cleaning tools, cooking paraphernalia, and everyday clothing.

Dead storage. Items relegated to the basement, attic, or garage (see pages 80–95) are said to be in "dead storage" because they are relatively inaccessible. Other dead storage areas in the house include hard-to-reach shelves, utility rooms, and awkwardly placed corner drawers. These are the places to store possessions used once a month or seasonally.

Closed or open storage?

What we lump together as storage can actually be divided into two categories: closed storage and open storage.

Closed storage conceals clutter—all of the not-so-decorative household items that should be kept out of sight. Cabinets and closets are typical of closed storage.

Open storage displays decorative articles, prized possessions, and all of the objects that you prefer leaving out. Open storage, such as shelving, can be intentionally placed at eye-level or against a plain background to focus more attention on what's stored.

Awkward corner space *becomes accessible with easy-opening, piano-hinged cabinet door. Architect: George Cody; Interior Designer: Stewart Morton.*

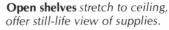

Open shelves *stretch to ceiling, offer still-life view of supplies.*

Partly-recessed shelf *units fit between widely-spaced supporting posts of non-bearing wall.*

Temporary or permanent storage?

You may be renting an apartment for only a few months or, at the opposite extreme, you may be building a house you plan to live in for the rest of your life. Consider whether storage should be permanent or temporary.

Temporary units. If you move frequently, you'll need storage that can be quickly and efficiently dismantled. Like permanent units, temporary units can be made of various materials, can be basic or customized, can be purchased or handmade. But what all portable units have in common is that they're either freestanding or fastened to walls only with screws or bolts, rather than nailed or framed in.

Built-ins. This permanent type of storage obtains the maximum amount of storage space with a minimum sacrifice of living area by utilizing between-the-studs square footage. Here are some advantages of using built-ins:

• *Units can be disguised or hidden.* Built-ins can have doors that match solid walls, invisible hinges, and unobtrusive door handles or pulls. Even if the units are attached snugly to an existing structure and project into the room, they can be finished to blend with their surroundings.

• *Size and shape are variable.* Built-in units can be designed to compensate for the deficiencies of any room. Blank wall space in some cases can be completely eliminated. Size and shape are especially open to variation when room dividers are made up of storage units.

• *Construction costs can be lowered.* If only the front of a built-in unit is visible, this will be the only place where finished materials are required. And since the attachment to walls or floor takes advantage of the room's basic structural strength, it may be possible to use a lighter grade of lumber and still have adequate support.

The greatest disadvantage of built-ins, of course, is their immobility.

FINDING STORAGE SPACE WITHOUT REMODELING

If you need new storage facilities but don't want to go to the trouble and expense of remodeling, consider some of these suggestions:

Switch or add furniture

Move your furniture around to make more wall space available. Rearranging furniture or removing paintings or other decorations can open up wall space where you can add new storage units.

You may also be able to use freestanding storage cases as pieces of furniture if they're well constructed and attractively finished. By attaching legs to a cabinet and using finished wood in construction, it can serve as an end table; a low chest covered with a cushion can become a window seat. Baskets, boxes, and trunks add interesting accents to rooms while they provide additional storage.

Re-think existing space

Reorganization of cabinet and closet interiors can open up space that is inadequately used. For example, adding adjustable shelves or converting shelving to trays or drawers may double the storage space within a unit. A special hook, rack, stand, pullout, rod, or hanger will accommodate almost every item that won't fit conveniently on a shelf or in a drawer. Most accessories are available in a wide variety of sizes or are adjustable. Regardless of the depth of a closet or the width of a cabinet, you can usually find an accessory to fit it.

Replace outdated units

Newer, more modern cabinets, shelving, and closets can mean more efficient storage. The materials new units are made of may be stronger, so you can keep heavier books on a standard length of shelving or hang more clothes on a new metal rod than a wooden one. A new storage item may also have design features that make it more efficient.

Easy to dismantle and set up again, versatile bookcase consists of simple vertical supports—slotted blocks of wood—holding horizontal shelves. Pieces projecting at intervals from the shelves fit into the slots. This bookcase can be built in different heights, widths, and lengths.

Completed built-in wall *divides into different shelf sizes and open sections to suit the possessions to be stored and displayed. Depths vary, but none of the units projects more than 3½ inches into the room. Small drawing board swings up, attaches to magnetic catch.*

Convert unused space

All areas out of traffic lanes and not being put to use can be converted to some sort of storage; every open wall is a potential storage wall or foundation for shelves or cabinets. A door can be outlined by bookshelves. The wall space below a window can be converted to a low storage cabinet. You can fill an alcove or similar wall irregularity with a closet or divide one room into two rooms by installing a room divider that's a storage unit. And under the stairs may be more adaptable storage space.

TYPES OF STORAGE UNITS

Once you've defined your particular storage needs, selecting the right kind of storage is the next step. This section examines components of storage units, moving from the smallest to the largest—hooks, shelves, bins, boxes, cabinets, and closets. Use it to pinpoint the best kind of storage for you—or the combination of kinds that will best meet your needs.

Hangers, hooks, pegs

One of the simplest forms of storage is the peg. It can be formed into all sorts of shapes to hold many different objects.

As you look through the illustrated idea sections grouped by rooms later in this book, you'll see peg-type hangers used for a variety of purposes—from supporting shelves to hanging a bicycle. Different types of hangers attach to walls or ceilings, cabinets, closets, and large drawers or shelves.

Perforated hardboard (pegboard) is a popular backing material into which you can insert hooks and hangers. The hangers that fit into the perforations come in metal and plastic and lock solidly into place.

Shelves

Any horizontal, flat, projecting surface that supports articles qualifies as a shelf. Shelves can be narrow or wide, long or short, thick or thin. They can be suspended from the ceiling, attached to or built into a wall, or be freestanding. Shelves may be openly displayed within a room or concealed within a unit.

For easy access, shelves should be less than 30 inches deep—less than 12 inches deep if stacked close together.

Shelves can be supported in various ways. They can rest on top of low tables or cabinets, be nailed or screwed directly into one, two, or three walls, or be supported by brackets, braces, angle irons, dowels, or clips.

With long shelving—in a unit such as a bookcase—it may be necessary to give added strength with extra supports placed at the midpoint of the span or at one or two-foot intervals.

Keep in mind the need to provide enough clearance between shelves to remove what's on them easily. Even with shallow storage, an inch or two over the tallest article is necessary to remove everything on the shelf; with deeper storage, the clearances needed increase proportionately.

Some shelves are movable; others are not. An important advantage to adjustable shelves is that they make maximum use of space—you can shift them to fit closely around their contents.

Because adjustable shelves are not permanently attached to supports but usually only rest on top of brackets, uneven loading or careless handling of objects on the shelf may cause it to wobble or tilt. On any shelf, if the articles stored are breakable, be doubly sure brackets are securely fastened to standards or firmly inserted in the wall.

You might find any of these three types of special shelving useful:

Half shelves. These are used to gain additional storage space in a closet or cabinet without altering the overall

Pairs of dowels (pegs) placed at intervals of 6 inches support rough-surfaced, adjustable shelves. Architect: Jack Selman.

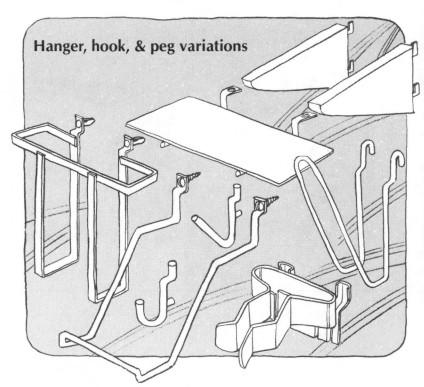

Hanger, hook, & peg variations

dimensions of the unit. They're often found in kitchen cabinets and in storage units for dinnerware but are useful in any storage area where waste space between stationary shelves is a problem. A half-shelf is the full width of the cabinet but only half the height and half the depth of a regular shelf.

Sliding shelves. Without wasting space, this type of shelf makes items stored in deep cabinets easily accessible. Sliding shelves are very convenient but not usually available as stock items, except as cutting boards in kitchen cabinets.

To support sliding shelves, you can obtain a pair of wooden or metal guides that are attached to two sides and provide an outside track for the shelf.

Pop-up shelves. You'll find these are useful in the kitchen for storing appliances, in a desk to accommodate a typewriter, or in a sewing center for hiding a sewing machine. In all cases, the operation is the same: the machine or appliance is per-manently stored on a shelf that is raised and lowered on metal hardware, eliminating lifting and carrying the machine from point of storage to point of use.

Hardware for a pop-up shelf can be purchased to fit almost any cabinet opening; the only requirements are vertical clearance and clearance for movement of the entire assembly. The amount of space needed for a pop-up is more than for other types of shelves because of the mechanism.

Bins and boxes

In this category are all those containers you reach into from above—baskets, tubs, and chests included. Many of them have lids; some don't.

Bins and boxes are ideal for bulk storage: to serve as laundry hampers, to store large quantities of dry foods, or to hold potting materials for garden work.

The main advantage of a tip-out bin is that it is easy to operate and exposes the full storage space when pulled open. You can reach the bottom of the bin easily and unload it with a minimum of effort. When closed, the bin keeps all items completely out of sight.

Steel tip-out bins intended to fit under a kitchen sink are available but only in limited styles and sizes. If you build a tip-out bin yourself, make it sturdy to avoid having the front or back pull away when the bin is opened suddenly. A tip-out bin will work satisfactorily only when the height of the opening to be filled is greater than the depth (see illustration). With equal dimensions or a greater depth than height, you will either have to insert a false back or design a special bin with a slanted front. In either case, not all of the cabinet space available can be used. Drawers or slide-out shelves would probably serve better.

Unless you're storing tall items, a box or bin can be partitioned efficiently with pull-out, divided shelves.

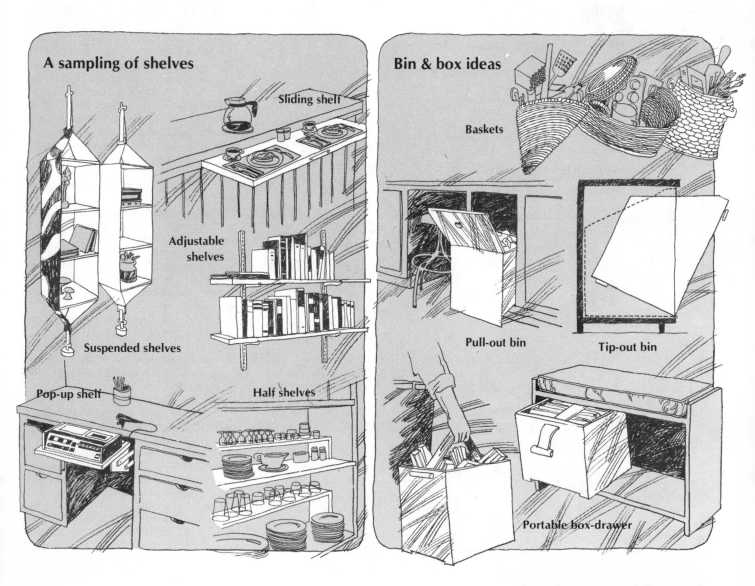

A sampling of shelves

Sliding shelf

Adjustable shelves

Suspended shelves

Pop-up shelf

Half shelves

Bin & box ideas

Baskets

Pull-out bin

Tip-out bin

Portable box-drawer

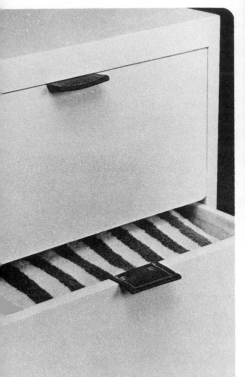

Flush drawers built into a wall open with finger openings on sides. Architect: Donald Gibbs.

Drawer pulls *made of leather tabs fit into shallow notch chiseled out of drawer edge.*

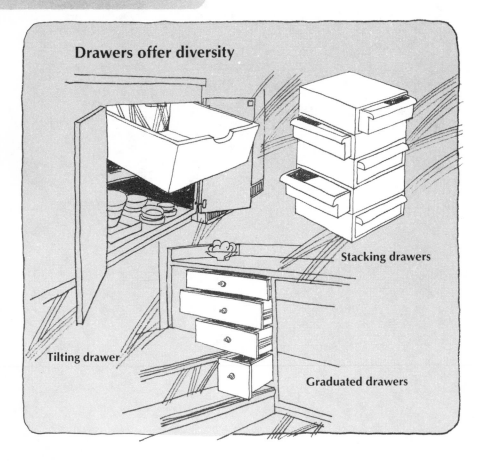

Drawers offer diversity

Tilting drawer

Stacking drawers

Graduated drawers

Drawers

Drawers are handy storage containers because they roll toward you, so are more accessible than most shelves. Ideally, drawers are easy to look and reach into; they open and close with little effort. Some kinds of drawers tilt down as they're pulled out. Drawers can be built into cabinets or chests, suspended under counters or tabletops, or made to slide on runners screwed onto shelves.

You should be able to stand directly in front of a drawer and open it to almost its full depth; it should be low enough for you to see to the bottom when it is open.

How large drawers can be is determined by their use, the materials they're made of, sliding system, size of load, and placement. Usually they should be not more than 12 inches high and 30 inches deep (the length of a long arm). Handles placed near the sides of the drawer but less than three feet apart give maximum pulling efficiency. Stops are important, particularly with large, heavy drawers, for keeping drawers from being pulled out of their casings.

Standard drawers are available in stock sizes, can be custom made to fit your particular needs, or can be built by you. Many kinds of containers can be used as drawers, as long as they have a bottom, sides, and a back. You can use the edge of some drawers as a fingergrip, order from the vast array of drawer pulls on the market, or devise your own drawer pulls.

Molded plastic, metal, or wooden drawers are available without frames, to be built in almost anywhere individually or in groups. Also sold are stacking drawers that interlock.

If you want to build drawers into a new house, you can buy complete chests of drawers or drawer cabinets. These drawers usually have sides and a back but may or may not have a top.

Drawer cases are chests without sides, back, top, or bottom. The framework surrounds several drawers. Less expensive than complete chests, they're built completely into a wall or have specially finished sides.

Building your own solid, trouble-free, standard drawers can be difficult. Professional cabinetmakers consider building drawers as one of their most difficult tasks, and most home craftsmen will share their feelings after working out the cutting, grooving, fitting, and special joints needed for standard drawers.

If you have drawers custom made, be prepared to tell the cabinetmaker the dimensions of the drawer opening, the type of front material you want, and your preferences—if any—about whether the front will be flush or lipped, whether front rails will be installed between the drawers, and how the drawer will be supported.

Guides are generally necessary to fit a drawer into its slot. To prevent wooden drawers from binding or sticking, metal guides are best. Or, if the guides are wood, smooth the edges of the guides and apply paraffin or wax. You can install a small drawer without tracks, if it fits loosely.

To partition a drawer, you can simply fill it with smaller containers. Or groove the bottom of the drawer—if it's not too thin—and insert dividers.

Cabinets and cupboards

Cabinets are excellent for tucking away clutter. They can be subdivided with shelves, drawers, smaller cabinets, boxes, and bins; they can be freestanding or built-in, open or fitted with doors.

Built-in wall cabinets can be installed on furring strips or attached directly to the wall studs. Some manufacturers of metal units provide a hanger bar; this is screwed into the wall studs at a specified height, and the cabinets have notches that fit on the bar. Stock cabinets come either with recessed or flush backs, suited to different methods of installation. Stock cabinets with drawers are usually more costly than ones fitted with shelves and a door.

Often the style of the cabinet is determined by its door (see pages 10–11). Another contributor to style is hardware. Manufacturers will sell cabinets without hardware holes so that you can place your own pulls or latches.

The best cabinets have these features: adjustable shelves in both wall and base units; drawers with smooth-gliding and safety-stop devices; and neatly detailed, smoothly finished interiors, shelves, and door backs.

Fillers, usually strips of wood or metal, are installed between cabinets to 1) fit cabinets into a too-big space, 2) compensate for a crooked or slanting wall, or 3) move a cabinet out away from a corner.

Kitchen cabinets. The two basic kinds of kitchen cabinets are wall and base types. Wall types are attached to the wall above a sink or elsewhere; base types are low and attached to the floor. In kitchen cabinets, you can obtain adjustable shelves, sliding shelves, pull-out trays, bins, and drawers of different sizes. Other possibilities are roll-around cabinets and cabinets designed for corners (see below). Special reinforced shelves for storing heavy case lots or bulk packages can be fitted into standard units. Base cabinets can be purchased either with or without countertops. For information on the features of different countertop materials, see the *Sunset* book *Planning and Remodeling Your Kitchen.*

These cabinets come in standard depths and variable widths (usually in multiples of three inches). Larger widths cost proportionately less than narrower.

Utility cabinets. Designed to hold cleaning implements or miscellaneous storage, utility cabinets come in stock sizes of 64 to 84 inches high, 24 to 30 inches wide, and 13 to 25 inches deep.

Corner cabinets. Where two rows of wall or base cabinets meet in a corner of a room, the storage space is often barely accessible. The hard-to-get-at pocket in the corner can be reserved for seldom-used items, or you can try one of the following suggestions for making this space more usable—although cabinet capacity will be reduced.

A good way to take advantage of the full space of a corner cabinet is to use a lazy susan. You can inspect the contents of the shelves at a glance and reach all the items by revolving the unit. The hardware isn't expensive, and installation in new cabinets is not difficult. For lazy susans 24 inches in diameter, 33 inches along each wall is needed for clearance; 30-inch lazy susans require 36 inches along each wall.

You can also install fixed, semicircular shelves within a corner cabinet or to the inside of a cabinet door so that they swing open when you open the door, rotating 360°. Sliding shelves can bring things out of the corner and into reach. Corner-shaped storage units, with a door cutting across the corner at a

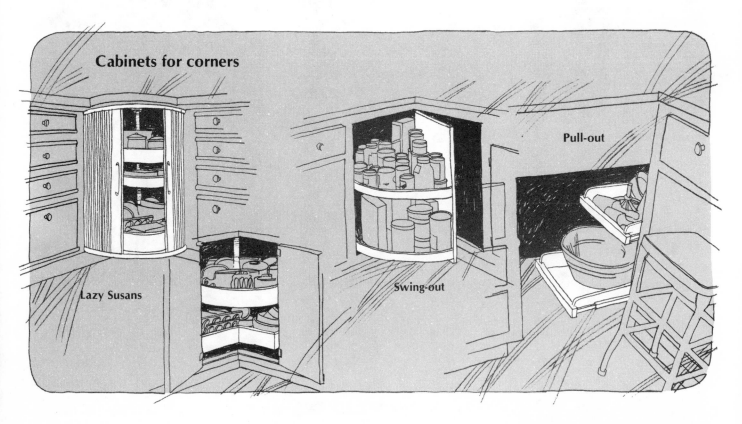

Cabinets for corners

Lazy Susans

Swing-out

Pull-out

45° angle, can help alleviate the access problem if the door is reasonably wide.

Closets

A closet, technically speaking, is a small room or recess for storing clothes, linens, and other items. Closets can be free-standing, anchored to the wall as cabinets often are, or built in.

The ideal closet depth for clothing is 24 to 30 inches; for linens and cleaning equipment, 20 inches; for most other articles, 12 to 16 inches. A closet 24 inches deep is adequate for handling most luggage, bedding, sporting gear, home movie projection equipment, and card tables and folding chairs. If your closet has a door of conventional height, try using the space above it for shelves.

In a new house, closets are usually custom-made to fill specific spaces as the house is being constructed. Prefabricated closets may be built of plywood,

hardboard, steel, or corrugated board. They're delivered either knocked-down or fully assembled and can be used free-standing or built in. Most often they measure 6 feet high, 21 inches deep, and up to 4 feet wide.

If you're adding a closet, one of the best places for it is in a corner—especially a cramped one. Alcoves alongside a fireplace or between pieces of furniture set against a wall form potential closet spaces.

Lighting a closet. A 75-watt incandescent bulb is adequate for illuminating most closets. If a closet is wide or a walk-in, use one or two 40-watt bulbs or fluorescent tubes. Mount light fixtures on the ceiling in a forward position that allows the most light to shine down past closet shelves. The bulbs don't need to be shielded. An extra convenience is a special switch that's recessed in the door jamb and automatically turns the closet light on and off as the door is opened

and shut. Cordless closet lights that operate on batteries are also available.

Ventilating and heating a closet. To keep a closet from becoming stuffy, install louvered or folding slat doors or bore holes in solid doors. A small exhaust fan in the ceiling, ducted to the outdoors, will bring in fresh air.

Mildew can be controlled with incandescent bulbs during humid weather. Small ozone lamps guard against mustiness. Cedar is traditionally used in closets to prevent damage from moths.

You can warm a closet slightly with incandescent bulbs; a small electric ceiling heater will do a more complete heating job. Or you could add a bathroom fixture incorporating exhaust fan, electric heater, and incandescent bulb to a closet ceiling.

Doors for cabinets and closets. Doors can be made of cloth, plastic, wood, metal, or glass; they can pivot, open on hinges, slide, roll, or fold. Doors keep

Bedroom office/closet, *formerly used for clothes, holds filing cabinet, desk, and storage shelves with room to spare. Architect: William Johnson.*

Hinged bookcase *swings out on casters concealed in toe space to reveal game, toy closet. Weight of case keeps it closed. Architect: Lorenzo Tedesco.*

dust out and, in most cases, conceal what's inside the storage unit.

Cabinet and closet doors can be either flush or lip. Flush doors may be desirable to give a uniform appearance to a series of units or to simplify installation with butt hinges; they also can be recessed or attached so they project slightly.

Doors are available in standard sizes from builders' supply houses; they come in a variety of facings and styles. If stock doors will not fit your cabinets, either have them cut at a cabinet shop or make them yourself to match the cabinet.

Latches of several different types and styles are sold, each featuring a different "trap." When selecting a catch, keep in mind the amount of work it will be required to do. Solid types that are not likely to loosen or bend and are not dependent on strict alignment to function properly are best for cabinets and closets in constant use.

Door knobs and pulls come in a multitude of styles and materials. They're available from building supply stores, specialty dealers, or can be made of materials you have on hand.

Here are five common types of doors:

• *Hinged doors* have long been the standard for cabinets and closets. The main advantage of swinging, hinged doors is that the entire closet or cabinet is opened with one movement. There are no tracks, ridges, or guides to collect dust and mar appearance, and the storage unit interior may be altered without removing or replacing the door. If in good working order, hinged doors require less effort to open and shut than other types of doors. You can use the surfaces of a hinged door for additional storage. However, these doors do require space in front of the storage unit for the door to swing open.

Use hinges that will support the full weight of the door and are strong enough to open and close without sagging or sticking.

When hanging doors, allow for freedom of movement both between paired doors and around hinges. Some carpenters judge the amount of space needed between double doors by inserting a paper match between them and then setting hinges. This clearance allows for free movement, preventing the doors from sticking together.

• *Pivot doors* can be built so the point at which they pivot is on the right, on the left, or in the center. With a center pivot, a swing span into the closet is necessary, taking up room that can't be used for storage. However, the back of a pivot door can be used for storage.

• *Sliding doors* on cabinets and closets can be quickly moved aside, take up minimum space, offer a clean, attractive surface, and—on better hardware—roll along quietly, without much of a push. They're often used on wide, shallow closets.

The main disadvantage of sliding doors is that only half the closet or cabinet can be opened at once when overlapping doors are used. Providing slots in the wall for the doors to slide into is costly but convenient.

• *Rolling doors* hang from the top of the opening on flanged tracks, attached by a hanger with a roller wheel to fit in the track and held in place with guides for the bottom of the door. Double ball-bearing nylon wheels (the most expensive type of mechanism) are efficient.

Tracks are available to fit doors from ¾-inch to 1⅜ inches thick. You can buy kits including all necessary hardware, screws, and directions.

Tambour doors, the type used on roll-top desks, pull upward instead of sideways. These doors can be adapted to many uses, especially where a work surface and supplies need to be concealed.

• *Folding doors* are stored in the opening they create and yet still open up most of the closet or cabinet at once. Stock doors are available in standard heights and widths.

Folding doors are available in steel, wood, plastic, and fabric. There are three general types: accordion or pantograph, hinged panels, folding slats (see below).

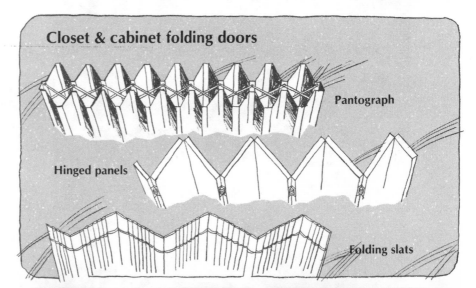

Closet & cabinet folding doors

Pantograph

Hinged panels

Folding slats

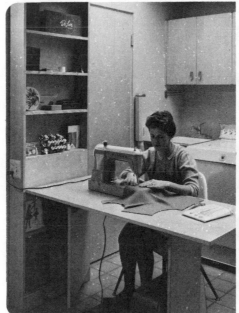

Fold-down cabinet door *serves as sewing or lunch counter when down, allows access to shelves behind it. Folded up out of the way, it takes up little room. Architects: Rushmore and Woodman.*

Modular shelves *use 12 by 16-inch plywood rectangles bolted together through 2 by 2s at joints. Can be taken apart easily, rearranged. Architect: Donald William MacDonald.*

Recycled spice cabinet *now stores extra clothing, makes handsome addition to upstairs hallway.*

Modular systems and combinations

A "modular system" uses standard-size components that fit together interchangeably. The components can be shelves, cabinets, drawers, record cubes, desks, bars, or other units to switch or substitute as you please. With most systems, practically any number or type of components can be combined, allowing you to design a storage unit that is just right for you.

Some modules stack like boxes, some hang on freestanding poles or uprights, some connect directly to each other, and some are attached to walls. Many hundreds of connector systems exist.

Although the modular principle is very versatile, you may want to combine other kinds of storage units on a different basis. For example, you might have bookshelves and cabinets of different sizes and styles already on hand that you can tie together effectively. Or sections that aren't modular might be combined with modular units to provide the specific type of storage you need. For instance, you might want a bedroom storage wall that's a combination of nonmodular clothes rods and shoe racks along with modular drawers, shelves, cabinets, and a vanity.

OBTAINING STORAGE UNITS

Once you have determined your storage needs and defined the various storage components that will fill those needs, the planning stages are over. Then it is time to act—to solve your storage problems by obtaining the right facilities. You can recycle old containers, build the units yourself, buy stock storage units, or hire a furniture designer or cabinetmaker to build custom units. A combination of these methods will work too: you might adapt old furniture for a new use, slightly rebuild stock cabinetry, or do the easy work yourself, hiring a cabinetmaker to complete the hardest parts for you.

Recycle older units

By turning outdated or outmoded containers and materials to new purposes, you can often create surprisingly attractive and functional storage units.

Look for things to recycle around your house or among articles other people are selling or giving away because they think the items are no longer useful. Simply by thinking beyond a container's original purpose, you can put its storage potential to work in unexpected ways.

The things you recycle needn't be antiques; containers of recent vintage that are out of style can become interesting again if put to a new use. An expandable hatrack used for hats is "old hat"; but if you hang skeins of yarn from it, it's fun.

New materials have made certain kinds of commercial containers obsolete to the businessman but not to the storage-hungry apartment dweller. Wooden crates formerly used for shipping fresh fruit can be stacked to make box-like bookcases; compartmented soft drink crates make efficient home office pigeonholes.

Whenever buildings, boats, or houses are dismantled, pieces emerge that can be reused. You can salvage old materials (such as weathered barn wood for shelves) or transfer a complete unit (such as a cabinet from a ship-shape galley) to your home.

Build units yourself

Practically anybody can make such simple storage units as bookshelves, pegs, hangers, and even some types of modest cabinets. Although this isn't always the easiest method, it is usually the least expensive.

Complete instructions for building the various storage ideas pictured in this book are not included, but the descriptions of different kinds of storage units (pages 6–12) will give you some idea of how difficult each is to build.

An excellent companion book to this volume is Sunset's *How to Make Bookshelves & Cabinets*. It gives precise, step-by-step directions for building various kinds of storage and display furniture.

Purchase stock items

Although furniture stores might be the first place you visit looking for storage units, they are not the only source. Some commercial office or factory-supply outlets handle items that can serve your storage needs. Most lumberyards and home-improvement centers carry unfinished cabinets and shelving.

Stock cabinetry can be installed quickly and inexpensively. The only problem is standardization—it is hard to find a stock cabinet that is tailored specifically to your needs or has out-of-the-ordinary design. You can save money and use your own customizing construction procedures by buying stock cabinetry precut and machined but unassembled and then assembling it yourself.

Order custom pieces

If you find that standard units don't fit your needs and don't want to build your own, you may want to hire a furniture designer or take your ideas to a cabinetmaker. Although usually the most expensive solution to storage needs, this approach assures that storage units will be tailored precisely to their purposes. You can usually locate a good craftsman in the yellow pages under "Cabinet Makers," "Woodworkers," or "Furniture—Custom Made."

If the job will be extensive, you might be wise to hire a remodeling or building contractor who will see it through to completion. Otherwise, be sure all the necessary work is carefully spelled out—including the hanging of doors, attachment of hardware, installation, and finishing.

Joining 1 by 2 lengths of fir created this collapsible bookcase. It measures 5 ½ inches deep—adequate for many books—and reaches from floor to ceiling.

Sturdy icebox *underneath counter makes pleasant change from usual cabinetry, insulates well.*

In the Kitchen

Placing utensils and supplies as close as possible to point of use is extremely important in a busy kitchen, where these items are used and reused daily.

The relative position of the stove, refrigerator, and sink is the most important factor in determining point of use. Take advantage of your kitchen's floor plan to organize supplies into specialized work centers for different tasks. See the Sunset book *Planning and Remodeling Kitchens* for specifics on setting up various types of kitchen work centers, such as a baking center. (If you have a planning desk in your kitchen, see pages 58–65 for storage ideas.)

Food storage

There's no foolproof way of determining how much food storage is needed in a typical household. Actually, your shopping schedule is more important than the size of your family in calculating food storage needs. For those who shop two or three times a week, a minimum amount of space may be adequate. On the other hand, considerable shelf space may be needed for those who bring home a carload of groceries to last a week or two.

Storing food for the convenience of the cook is often the best arrangement, but certain foods keep better when stored at a distance from heat and moisture.

Pantries most efficiently store large quantities if the shelving is about 8 inches deep. This depth allows for one or two-deep storage of regular-sized cans and dry goods and eliminates removing several items to get to the one in the back. The shelves should be firmly supported on cleats or brackets. Width and height of the shelf openings depend on the size of the item to be stored. If the pantry is limited to canned goods, slight-

WALK-IN PANTRY

Preparing meals *goes faster with all ingredients and equipment a step or reach away. Two more areas—for meal planning and for assembling meals—increase kitchen efficiency. Designer: Judy Perry.*

Two roll-tops *installed in a remodeled kitchen conceal a planning desk and a section of counter. White-tiled warming counter, wine rack, and additional cabinets above add to this kitchen wall's versatility.*

ly sloping shelves can feed the cans one at a time to the front of the shelf (rimmed with a small piece of molding to keep cans from falling off).

SLOPING SHELVES

A pantry used for home-canned foods should be cool, dry, and well ventilated. If dry foods are stored in glass jars, they must be kept in a dark and cool place. Certain fruits and vegetables are also best kept in a cold, dark place, which can be a pantry, cooler, or even a cellar (see page 81).

A freezer operates at maximum efficiency when its contents are continually rotated. Space should be assigned first to heavier and more expensive foods and to ones that can't be preserved as well any other way. It's best to label and date packages of food and to store similar foods together. Six cubic feet of freezer space per family member is about right. Operating costs per pound of food are less if the freezer is kept at least three-quarters full.

Herbs and spices should, ideally, be kept away from heat, moisture, and light. The handiest place for them is close to the food preparation center, turned so you can read the labels easily. Jar lids and can tops should be kept tightly closed to prevent volatilization of these aromatic substances. Popular commercial units for spice storage include auxiliary shelves, special cabinets, and revolving spice racks with two or three tiers.

Wine can be stored on any shelf, closet, or corner, as long as a few requirements are met. One is that the wine should be away from direct sunlight. Also, there should be no vibration or movement. The temperature should remain fairly even—best is between 50° and 60°. And the bottles should be placed horizontally on their sides or tilted down slightly to keep the corks moist and airtight.

Compartmentalized commercial racks are widely available, or you could use drainage tiles or fiber storage tubes in a strong frame. Even cardboard liquor cartons, on their sides, can be used as wine storage units.

Utensils and appliances

Making the storage unit fit the item to be stored is especially important with cooking utensils because they come in so

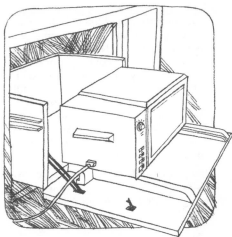

TRACKS ON CABINET DOOR

Tightly organized *in separate units, section of kitchen resembles ship's galley, efficiently combines storage. Architect: William W. Kirsch.*

Recessing adjustable shelf tracks *in posts makes it possible to install heavy butcher block counter and shelf on irregular wall. Architect: Edmund Ong.*

Two-unit hot plate *slides out for morning coffee and between-meal snacks. Architect: Sidney E. Snyder.*

Baskets in drawer of sewing machine cabinet incorporated into remodeled kitchen keep silverware organized.

many distinctive shapes. Specially shaped drawers, dividers, and shelves are available in commercial kitchen cabinetry.

Whenever possible, it's best not to stack kitchen tools—they're harder to remove and replace when piled on top of each other.

Store portable appliances adjacent to the work area and on the same level whenever possible. These time and work savers do take up counter space when stored this way, but since most of the work done on a 24-inch kitchen counter is toward the front, the rear portion can often be used for storage. Placed near an electrical outlet, the appliance can be concealed by flexible, roll-back, or sliding doors when not in use.

Hang pots and pans—especially those used every day—for the most functional storage. Hung on separate hooks close

grooves or held by cleats in a cabinet or drawer, they will store a large number of flat items. Be sure that the cabinet or drawer in which you install vertical dividers is deep enough to handle your largest trays. Also make sure that the storage unit will open far enough to permit easy removal of the utensils.

Store knives separately to protect the blades from nicks and dulling. If you are remodeling or planning a new kitchen, you may want to consider a chopping block with slots to hold knives vertically. Or, you could add a slotted strip of wood to the bottom of a cabinet shelf or in a shallow drawer.

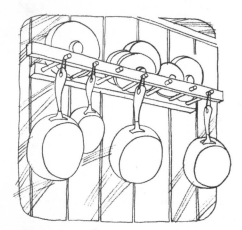

PAN RACK

to the range, they can be reached easily (see page 6). Commercial sliding brackets made specifically for pots and pans are another good idea. You could place these brackets in a cabinet below counter-top burners for easy accessibility.

Hooks or shallow racks are the best storage units for pot lids, but you can also purchase stock lid holders in varying sizes. Or you may prefer to use vertical dividers in a deep drawer.

Stand flat pieces, such as trays and cookie sheets, in vertical dividers. Set in

Roll-around cart fits neatly under kitchen island; drawers, horizontal slots hold serving equipment. Architect: Otto Poticha.

Mid-kitchen peninsula combines structural drawers and cabinets with section of open shelves, compartments. Architect: Vladimir Ossipoff & Associates.

Revolving spice jars, *their lids screwed to a 4-sided wooden bar, fit inside chest.*

Block of wood, *drilled with 2-inch holes, makes a solid yet movable spice holder. Designer: James P. Livingston.*

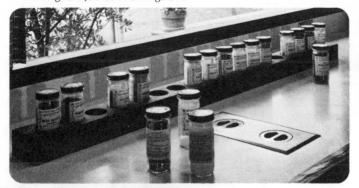

Five ways to store spices & herbs

Swing-down spice rack *utilizes small space at end of upper cabinet. Shelves on hinged door double capacity; thin wood strips hold jars. Designer: Ned Doll.*

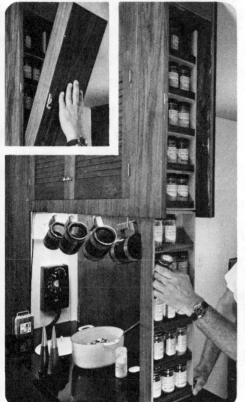

Still-life quality of spice jars *and canisters receives emphasis from an antiqued gold frame; gallery light above adds authentic touch.*

Wood strip *(sold as support for fiberglass roof) glued into drawer at an angle supports spice jars. Designer: Russell Roote.*

Pantries...
for quantity storage

Perforated hardboard *lines door of full-height pantry. Architect: A. Jane Duncombe.*

Widening *into work counter, open shelves disappear behind doors. Architects: Trogdon-Smith.*

Swinging shelf *section makes efficient use of ample space, eliminates rummaging for staples in rear of deep shelves. Architects: Groom, Blanchard, Lamen & MacCollin.*

Corner pantry *displays half its storage on the doors; all items stay visible and accessible. Architects: Hyun and Whitney.*

Keeping food fresh

Slits in door *ventilate this cabinet used for dry cereals and prevent air inside from becoming too warm. Heat diffusing from adjacent wall oven keeps cereals crisp.*

Cool storage cupboard *with bottom section constructed like a traditional cooler opens to the outside of the house for ventilation. Roll-out tray holds vegetable bins.*

Unexpected space for food

Vertical *units pull out to full depth of cabinet, exploit every bit of space. Shelves are lipped.*

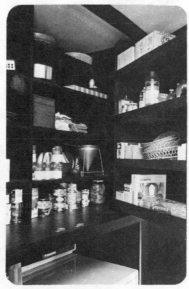

Small, compact *pantry is above washer and dryer. Architect: Charles Metcalf.*

Shallow shelves *hold one row of cans; cart fits behind them under counter. Architect: Robert Lawton.*

Storing wine
in the kitchen

At room temperature, *most wine will keep up to a year—as long as other storage requirements are met. Compartmentalized wall rack groups different types of wine; more compartments could be added.*

Stacked *mailing tubes, on shelves supported by concrete blocks, contain wine.*

Honeycombed, *see-through wine rack forms top of kitchen room divider. Architect: Fred H. Field.*

Drawer *for cooking wines conceals behind a door. Designer: Janean.*

Nick-proof knife storage

Magnets *hold these knives in place, keeping blade shape visible. Designer: David Tucker.*

Slot *cut in shelf trim makes simple knife holder, keeps knives within easy reach. Designer: Harold Ogle.*

Pull-out *knife rack's slotted top separates the sharp blades. Architect: Raymond Kappe.*

Accessories that save time

Damp dishtowels *dry by the heat of a 75-watt bulb. Designer: Janean.*

Bins *on extension glides pull out from under a sink. Designer: Harper Poulson.*

Wet dishes *dry themselves on slotted rack above sink. Designer: Al Garvey.*

Holders *cut from mailing tubes, covered with adhesive-backed paper, keep cords free of tangles. You may want identifying labels.*

You can conceal small appliances...

Ball casters *roll cabinet-cart out from under permanent counter. Portable unit stores baking gear, provides extra counter space.*

Sandwich center *makes meal preparation easier. Toaster plugs into outlet at back of slide-out shelf; cutting board fits over cutlery drawer. Architect: Robert E. Small.*

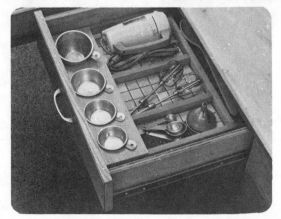

Tiled sections *of utensil drawer are easily cleaned; dividers form compartments sized for small tools.*

Built into a drawer, *power unit for blender and mixer plugs into an outlet at the back. Closing drawer protects unit from dust and crumbs. Accessories store alongside unit.*

...put them on, in, or underneath

Swing-up door *hides oven and mixer at convenient counter height. Appliance garages such as this one keep kitchen tools handy and unobtrusive. Designers: John and Mary Ellen Wilkins.*

Disappearing slicer *attached to a counter cutout folds down into a cabinet, leaving a flat-surfaced counter. Square section of countertop swings up and over on hinges; the slicer is permanently mounted to the bottom side of the counter cutout. Architect: Marvin Witt, Jr.*

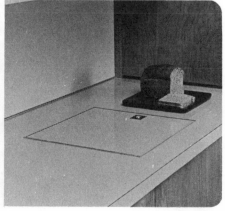

Places for pots, pans, & utensils

Inside cabinet doors, *shallow shelves with deep lips store pan lids and other miscellany. Setback shelves permit clearance as doors close.*

Partitions in drawer *separate pan lids; drawer sides were grooved before assembling. Architect: Arnold Gangnes.*

Divider *combines full-length shelving section at left with vertical storage below. Architect: A. Quincy Jones.*

Sliding *perforated hardboard panels fit neatly above refrigerator. Designers: Mayta & Jensen.*

Pull-out bin *makes graters and strainers easy to reach; center partition doubles hanging space for irregular shapes.*

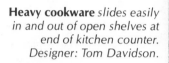

Heavy cookware *slides easily in and out of open shelves at end of kitchen counter. Designer: Tom Davidson.*

Visually interesting *collection of pots and pans hangs near table, takes up little space. Architect: Robert Herman.*

Out of cook's way *yet easy to reach, cookware hangs from hooks on bicycle-wheel version of overhead rack.*

Grooved sides *of cupboard within a cupboard hold sliding shelves at adjustable levels.*

In the Dining Area

Fine china, serving pieces, and glassware are traditionally put on display in the dining room, but many dining room storage principles can also be applied to everyday dishes kept in the kitchen or the breakfast area. Accessibility and breakage prevention are the most important factors in setting up storage for dishes and glassware; table linens need to be kept wrinkle-free.

For displaying tableware, glass or plastic doors on cabinets can be decorative and have the added advantage of protecting against dust. Of course, open shelving can also be attractive. Unless open shelves are out of the reach of careless hands, though, the display can be costly. If open shelving is best for your particular situation, add rims to the shelves and allow a 1-inch safety space between stored items and the shelf edge.

Dinnerware

Stacking — generally one of the greatest errors associated with storage—can be an efficient method of storing dinnerware. Stacking of four, six, or eight pieces all the same size and shape not only saves space, but makes setting the table easier. Don't stack valuable pieces too high.

Rely on uniformity of dinnerware pieces—make the storage units the exact size of the items to be stored and stack identical pieces. Short on space? A shelf 12 inches deep will hold all your dishes—except for larger platters and serving pieces.

If you don't have the space for one-deep storage, pull-out shelves could be the answer. Pull-out trays made of plastic or rubber and of varying sizes can be easily installed in most cabinets.

If you have extra room, commercial vinyl-coated wire racks for vertical storage can give easy access to your dishes.

Slant oversize pieces on tilted shelves on a 12-inch base, or store them flat on a shelf 16 inches deep. By adjusting the degree of slant, platters up to 16 inches can be stored on a 12-inch shelf. Or, you could try leaning larger pieces against the back wall of a cabinet.

Although not as convenient as other methods, this may be the only answer if space is limited. A protecting strip of quarter-round molding is all that is needed to prevent sliding.

Don't pile cups—although the size of cups is fairly uniform, the shape is not. Stacking in this case isn't the best storage method, for several reasons: appearance is messy; handles often protrude above the drinking level and the cups will not balance evenly; a handle can be broken or the rim chipped while removing one cup; and the temptation is to remove them by stacks, with dropping a likely result.

Again, one-deep storage can be the answer. Half-shelves work as well for cups as for the glassware. Or, you may prefer to hang cups on special racks that slide out of a cabinet, or hooks mounted on the bottom of a cabinet shelf.

Glassware

Everyday glassware—often made up of odd sizes and broken sets—is used at

Versatile china cabinet functions as room divider for dining room, extra seating for living room. Designer: William K. Stout.

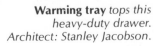

Warming tray tops this heavy-duty drawer. Architect: Stanley Jacobson.

such a rapid rate that easy access overshadows any consideration for appearance. The uniformity of better glassware enables you to store a maximum number of pieces in a small area, but arranging the shelves to eliminate breakage can be tricky. Here are some suggestions for handling the features of most glassware:

Eliminate deep storage to cut down on breakage. This can be done simply by dividing the glasses between the front 6 inches of two shelves, eliminating

SHALLOW CURVED SHELF

fumbling for that favorite glass which always seems to be behind two or three others. An alternate method is to install half-shelves against the back walls of the cabinets. In this way, flat dinnerware can be stored below the shelves and yet not interfere with removal of the glasses.

Also, consider the possibilities of constructing a between-the-studs cabinet or reframing a cabinet that once held an ironing board. This type of cabinet will provide shelves that are about 4 inches deep—an adequate space for one-deep storage.

Make the shelves adjustable to reduce waste space. One or 2 inches of space above the stored glasses is all that is required for easy removal. You will find that several different sets of glasses can be stored in one shallow cabinet.

Table linens

The major problem in storing tablecloths and napkins is that they tend to become wrinkled from their own weight and the shifting that occurs when one item is removed from the bottom of a stack. So, avoid heavy stacking.

Adjustable or pull-out shelving in existing closet or cabinet space not only cuts down on wasted open space but also allows you to store each linen set separately. Replacing clean linens or removing them for use won't disturb the other

BIN WITH DOWELS

sets. Pull-out shelves have the added advantages of making all pieces visible and easy to reach.

Swing-out towel racks can be installed in a closet or an open section of a cabinet. Linens are easy to remove or replace on the movable arms.

Cardboard tubing or cylinders, obtainable from a fabric store, permit you to roll your table linens around the tubes, secure them with pins, and store.

Flannel-lined closet *stores silver: serving pieces on shelves, flatware in drawers. Pieces of flannel drape over each shelf opening to keep air out. Architects: Pearson and Wuesthoff.*

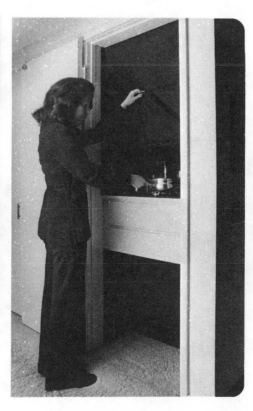

Adding third slotted track *permits use of shallower middle shelf and storage of taller items in front.*

Well-planned passthroughs

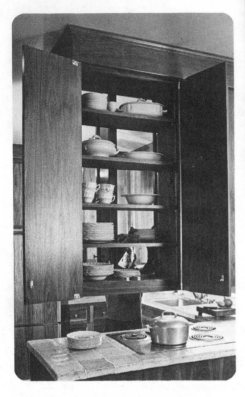

For casual convenience, *hinged panel resting on pull-out support provides counter space between kitchen and dining area. On formal occasions, closed passthrough presents a solid wall to dining room. Architect: Theodore T. Boutmy.*

Overhead passthrough *cupboard makes dish storage and table setting easier. Designer: Janean.*

Ways to store glassware

Glasses line up *on open shelves, mugs on hooks below. Architect: Robert Herman.*

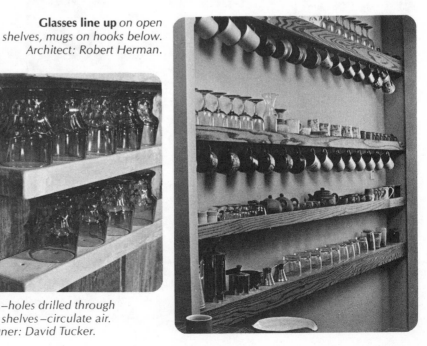

Extra glasses *disappear into wall-hung cabinet. Designer: R. L. Baumfeld.*

Vents—*holes drilled through these shelves—circulate air. Designer: David Tucker.*

Finishing nails *outline unusual shapes of stainless pieces, keep them from becoming jumbled.*

Drawer between counter levels *holds napkins, silverware, miscellany used at eating counter. Architect: Morgan Stedman.*

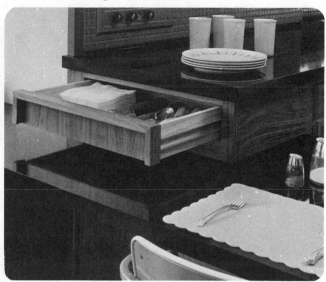

Organizing your silverware

Easy-to-get-to *silver chest rests on a convenient pull-out shelf equipped with stops. Wood strips nailed to the top of the shelf fit snugly inside a second set nailed to the bottom of the chest, keep chest from sliding off. Designer: Henry Lace.*

Hang, roll, or stack table linens

Island/divider *between kitchen, family dining room combines sliding trays for linens and flat tableware on dining side with kitchen drawers.*

Rolled around dowels *to minimize wrinkling, tablecloths store in slotted frame inside a drawer.*

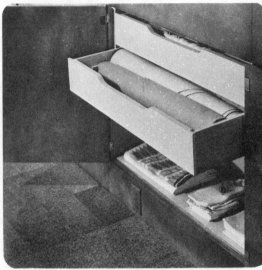

Linens *hang wrinkle-free on rods in cabinet between dining area and the kitchen. Architect: Charles Chamberland.*

Swing-out towel racks *keep table linens smooth; movable arms make the linens easy to remove.*

Table setting conveniences

Compact storage compartment designed to hold glassware, linens in shallow drawers, and dishes opens to family eating area. On kitchen wall behind compartment stand open shelves, cabinets for more dishes.

Lazy Susans secured to shelves below counter make dishes easy to reach from two sides. Architects: Hobbs Fukui Associates.

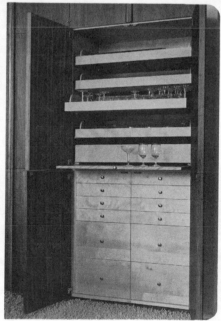

Floor-to-ceiling dining room storage wall consists of sections that open independently. The pull-out shelves and trays increase dinnerware accessibility, forestall accidents. Architects: Benton & Park.

Shelves hold accouterments; louvers hide them from guests. Architect: James Oliver.

In the Living Room or Family Room

Well-planned storage in the rooms you do your living in—family room, den, and formal living room—can add design, color, and atmosphere. Some of a family's most frequently used possessions—books, magazines, stereo, and television—are often stored in these rooms. Firewood, games, extra tables, or home movie equipment are also kept in these living areas.

Bookshelves are versatile

Bookshelves can be freestanding, built-in to fill an open corner or unused section of wall, used as a room divider, or combined with music equipment. Bookcases hung high on a wall avoid complications of furniture arrangement and bring color and pattern to eye level. Bookcases placed low on a wall leave space for wall hangings or paintings. Perhaps a bookcase could frame a window. If you concentrate your books on one wall of your living room, you can gain a strong decorative element and make the room warm and inviting. And bookcases can be combined effectively with general storage units.

Two shelf sizes suffice for books, which measure 8 to 10½ inches in height and about 5½ to 8½ inches in width. Bookshelf space should be a minimum of 9 inches high and 8 inches deep for books of average size. For larger volumes, a shelf 12 inches high and 12 inches deep will usually be adequate. Adjustable shelving may be the answer for adapting bookcases to fit a wide range of book sizes. Width of the shelving depends on the amount of wall space you have available and the number of volumes to be stored. Estimate 8 to 10 average-sized books to each running foot of shelf. Titles should be well lighted and readable.

Plan for easy access, remembering that a shelf 6½ feet above the floor will probably be the highest an average-sized person can reach without standing on a ladder. The space above can be fitted with doors for bulk storage cabinets, or used as display niches.

The three or four lowest shelves may also be inconvenient for you. General storage cabinets built in the lower 30 inches of a bookcase can be very prac-

Niches in divider *between living room and family room frame art objects, divide books; wet bar fits into a triangular cutout. Designer: William K. Stout.*

tical. Or you may want to convert this space to deep shelving for atlases and other large volumes. The top of the lowest section can extend out to form a counter for work or browsing.

Storing magazines

Magazines are seldom read in one sitting. They tend to fall where they're used —on tables, desks, chairs, counters— so they'll be handy to pick up again later on. Unfortunately, this temporary convenience often results in long-term inconvenience as more magazines and other items are piled one on another.

Flat shelves usually present no problems. The main point is to keep the shelves wide and deep enough to handle the largest magazines to be stored. Just measure the issues that come into your home every week or month and design your storage units to fit these issues. Store them bound edge out so you can find the one you're interested in.

Tilted shelves that expose titles offer another popular and easy solution to storing magazines, and they can be used for paperbound books, too. This type of shelving can be placed in regular bookcases or you can convert an entire section of wall to magazine storage. Not only will this keep order, but the changing covers add a bright touch of color to the room if they're consistently attractive.

Vertical racks can store a surprisingly large number of magazines while taking

PORTABLE MAGAZINE RACK

up a minimum of space. A rack can be made to fit into even the narrowest unused wall section.

Magazine binders—available through many publishing companies—usually hold either 6 or 12 issues. Or you can make your own to hold a different number of copies. Binders are made of various materials: plywood covers will keep magazines neat and will stand up through long use, but you may find that laminated plastic is adequate for your needs.

Fireside storage

A fireplace needs fuel—lots of it. A portable woodbox may be all you need if the fireplace isn't used very often. But built-in wood storage can eliminate unwelcome trips to the woodpile.

A fireside locker with a door that opens outside or into the garage can be a convenient arrangement. This structure must fill Uniform Building Code requirements as well as your needs. The Building Code requires that a woodbox opening into a garage or carport have a solid-core door with a self-closing apparatus—even if the carport is open on three sides.

A cantilevered hearth or recessed hearth often provides the easiest solution to storing firewood. Orderly stacking will eliminate the need for an enclosure. But if you want the wood to be covered, a simple fire screen will do the job.

A cabinet in a wall near the fireplace is another storage method. You can balance the cabinet door design with other

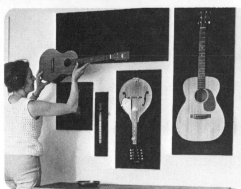

Storage wall extends from kitchen, includes desk, TV, stereo, card tables, folding chairs. Outdoor section has sink, counter, storage for furniture, games. Architect: Edward Sullam.

Shapes, sizes *of stored objects determined proportions of the compartments in this portable shelf system. Designer: Jeffrey A. Hipp.*

Black burlap *covering each plywood panel makes an effective backdrop for instruments' polished wood.*

room cabinets or conceal it in wood paneling. Take a look around your fireplace area for possible hideaways. Perhaps the bottom part of a bookcase could be utilized.

Woodboxes should be wide or deep enough to hold the largest logs you plan to use. As an added convenience, you might want to build a small shelf to hold matches, paper, or gloves. Dividing the cabinet into two sections helps to keep the kindling separated from the logs.

Preventing beetles from making their homes in your firewood is a major consideration. Here are two methods of beetle prevention: 1) spray the storage box with a household insecticide, and 2) line the box with sheet metal.

Stereo equipment

Planning storage of a finely tuned music system presents a unique situation: the components must be stored where they will have proper ventilation and easy accessibility, yet the location must also be excellent from the standpoint of listening enjoyment. Possible locations include between the wall studs, the interior of a closet with a perforated panel or even a small fan for ventilation, or in a bookshelf or cabinet. Many receivers, tuner-amplifier combinations, and speakers are designed attractively for open display. Open placement assures outstanding ventilation.

A separate receiver generates more heat than any other component so must be well ventilated. Unvented, it can get hot enough to blister a cabinet's finish.

The turntable's chief requirement is a stable, level platform. Relatively little vibration can cause a needle to jump the track on a record. The turntable will probably be your largest single component, requiring a shelf about 16 inches square.

Speakers need no ventilation. Whether your speakers are housed in one or more cabinets, the enclosure must be absolutely solid. The proper material to cover the speaker opening can be obtained from sound equipment dealers.

Records and tapes

If possible, store your collection of records and tapes next to the equipment they're played on—but protect them from heat (windows, amplifiers, heaters). Records are heavier than books; tapes and books weigh about the same.

A cabinet shelf 13 inches high and as deep will allow you to stand all records on edge. A shelf 8 inches high will be adequate for storing most tapes. Simple hardboard dividers placed every few inches make it easy to find records. Partitioned shelves within a closet could provide you with a similar organization. Even a bookshelf can suffice for storing records, provided it is deep enough.

Pull-out bins can be placed on pull-out shelves or simply set on a shelf for easy removal. You can store records and tapes label-side out in these.

SIMPLE RECORD BIN

Commercial cabinets or stands are available in various sizes and shapes. Many have wire separators to hold the records on edge.

Television & home movie gear

If you feel that a television screen, like a movie screen, should be hidden when there's no show on, you may be interested in these ideas.

A television cabinet can be designed and built in a number of ways. This need not be a large, permanently located fixture—a small roll-around cabinet for a portable television set may

be sufficient. The top of the cabinet can also serve as an extra table top or serving tray. Or you could cut out a portion of wall between two rooms and insert a portable TV set that can swivel around to face either room; you may wish to have a small door on each side.

Before you embark on a project of your own, consult a television technician to get his recommendations for proper set ventilation. Ideally, the television enclosure should be vented at the bottom, back, and top. In snug situations, you may have to install a small fan that operates when the set is on.

Home movie gear varies widely in size and shape. Compartmentalizing prevents damage to valuable equipment. Film should be located away from temperature extremes—a uniform temperature of 70° is best.

One of the favorite spots to hang a roll-down screen is behind a window valance. An exposed ceiling beam can also be used to conceal a permanent screen from one side.

PROJECTOR STAND

Ladder of dowels *14 feet high, built into center of tall bookcase, brings books, objects on top shelves within reach.*

Utilizing every square foot

Angular space *under stairs accommodates many books. Architects: Edwards-Pitman.*

Displayed in front *of a window, collection of artifacts fills adjustable shelves. Arrangement can screen a view without significant loss of daylight.*

Enclosed *by adjustable shelves in box-like framing, window seat becomes inviting, efficient storage area.*

By the fire

Hearth extends *30 inches into 18-inch-high niche for storing wood under set-in prefabricated metal fireplace. Architects: Davidson/Hughes/Franke.*

Grillework *conceals a stereo speaker and convenient wood storage box; rear of box opens to outside. Architect: Ron Wilson.*

Living room features *a built-in vertical slot for wood, wall of shelves, and fireside sofa. Architect: Alan Liddle.*

Inside freestanding cabinet, *canvas wood tote keeps sawdust and litter from spilling onto the floor. Plywood bottom liner in tote makes carrying kindling easier. Architect: James A. Miller.*

Putting away folding tables & chairs

Resurfaced *with a patterned, foam-backed vinyl fabric, folding card table makes a handsome decoration to hang on a wall.*

Beneath counter *separating breakfast area from family room, compartment accepts card table's height, depth.*

End wall opens *to show closet divided into sections for stereo equipment, folding chairs, and card tables.*

Some bookshelf variations...

Full wall *of bookshelves, punctuated by louvered window, stores large number of volumes. Architect: George Cody; Interior Designer: Stewart Morton.*

Shelves *above hall cabinets extend around corner. Architect: Vladimir Ossipoff.*

Ledge *serves as seat for browsers. Architect: Vladimir Ossipoff.*

Low shelves built *into wall put books within easy reach of a comfortable chair. Architects: Walker & McGough.*

...formal & informal

Tracks *and brackets attach to ceiling-high posts. Rubber chair glides cushion the posts against the ceiling; adjustable appliance leveling feet keep posts securely in place. Architect: Stuart Goforth.*

Wedged between floor *and ceiling, bookcase-display wall consists of shelves mounted on shelf tracks inset in pairs of vertical 2 by 4s. Designer: Paul Smith.*

Wall display *has rounded corners on vertical members, permanently secured shelves. Stiffeners at back of shelves strengthens them, holds them out from uneven wall. Architect: A. O. Bumgardner.*

Tall books *stand upright in shelves fitted under beam. Architects: Jones and Emmons.*

Portable bookcase, *light enough to screw onto a wall, holds small books. Top, bottom boxes attach to wall; center box pulls out. You could turn boxes, change dimensions.*

Clean-lined cube table *has room for magazines. Stack or line up more cubes for additional storage. Architects: Harry and Helen Som.*

Four ways to store magazines

Extending around corner, *library wall includes rack, low shelves for magazines. Architect: Henrik Bull.*

Glued and nailed *together, then nailed to trim, rack fits into small section of wall. Designer: Russell V. Lee.*

Tall magazine cabinet *acts as room divider and framework for built-in seating behind it. Hardboard shelves fit at intervals of four inches. Architect: Paul Sterling Hoag.*

Television *can be concealed behind flush doors; similar doors directly above open to more storage for miscellany.*

Toning down the television

Counter *houses bar sink, laundry, storage cabinets, television that faces family room. Architect: Raymond Lloyd.*

Casters *on piece of hardboard rotate this television to face almost any part of living room. Protruding pin under set rides in slot cut in the hardboard so television doesn't roll out of cabinet. Closed, cabinet defines the corner.*

Low cabinet forms framework of built-in couch. Three center sections open at top, contain turntables, controls; two on ends have doors, house records, tapes. Architect: Paul Sterling Hoag.

Sliding trays for turntable, albums fit inside tall, narrow cabinet that conceals behind a flush door. Architect: George Cody; Interior Designer: Stewart Morton.

Record cube stores standard-sized jackets in 13¼-inch openings on four sides; cube swivels on a 6-inch turntable.

Stacked-box unit has solid vertical shelf ends, rests on brackets set into tracks mounted on wall studs. Architect: Stuart Goforth.

...concealed or out in the open

Tapes fit neatly *into four compartments of narrow pull-out drawer. A larger drawer conceals records.*

Rolling *shelf-cart fits snugly into closet, using all available space; pulls out for access to wires connecting with speakers.*

Home movie equipment

Pressing button raises and lowers *this screen with its roll mechanism hidden behind a wood container painted the same color as the ceiling beams. Architect: Burr Richards.*

Slide carousels store *on shelves above, below projector shelf that pulls out for slide shows. Electrical outlet built into cabinet keeps projector cord neatly out of the way; narrow shelf above projector stores accessories. Architects: Raider, Strachocki, and Towbin.*

In a Child's Room

If their storage units are attractive and easy to use, children will be more likely to actually use them. Try giving cupboards and cabinets a toylike appeal with clever design and decoration. Place storage units low enough so that children can easily reach them.

Keep in mind, too, that a child may be using the same room for a number of years. Storage units should be keyed to cope with changes in a child's size and interests and to stand up to wear and tear.

A general rule for making storage units flexible is to keep away from built-ins. However, built-ins can be your answer if they are equipped with adjustable shelves and adjustable clothes rods. Otherwise, freestanding chests of drawers and closets are easier to modify as the child grows older. The same is true with desk and work or play areas. Simply adding more work surfaces and standard storage units saves effort in the long run, particularly when shelves and compartments are adjustable.

Children's clothing

A dream of parents is to have their child take care of his own clothes storage. Impossible? Not if you design the storage unit so the child has no trouble opening the door or reaching hangers and replacing them. Also, drawers that are low enough to reach into encourage developing the habit of tidiness.

Design the clothes closet to allow for the height and reaching distance of your child. For children three to five years old, place the clothes rod 30 inches off the floor. When the child grows older, raise the rod to 45 inches. Consider the depth of a closet also. It doesn't need to be the full 24 inches required for adults. But, if it is this depth from the start, the closet won't need enlarging when the child wants the full space.

Provide for folded clothes (or flat ones) with a low chest of drawers or open shelves. The more shallow the drawers, the better. This shallowness will prevent heavy loading and the child will have no trouble pulling the drawers open. Also, every item in the drawer will be easy to see.

Solve shoe storage problems in the easiest way by purchasing a commercial shoe rack that fits neatly in a closet. Or, you can build a simple rack, partitioned box, or series of shelves that fits under hanging clothes. Make the spaces large enough for bigger shoes as feet grow.

Keeping toys off the floor

The difficulty in storing toys is that they come in a dazzling array of sizes and shapes. Not only do the storage units have to be large enough to handle a variety of toys, but they should be flexible enough to accommodate the changing interests of children.

Make storage boxes simple. A practical way of doing this is to use heavy cardboard boxes, painted in bright hues or covered with boldly designed wallpaper

Toys in cages with dowel bars, bulletin board-chalkboard that hinges down to form a train board, and swing-out bins below add to child's storage wall.

or giftwrap. When the boxes become beaten and bedraggled, replace them with new containers. Other kinds of storage boxes can be built of many different materials, set on casters, or fitted underneath a bed or window seat.

Whatever sort of toy box you use, be sure to keep it low enough. A child often plays on the floor, and a shallow box will make it easier to get toys out and put them away. Storage boxes shouldn't be too large, because the toys piled underneath can break. Also, a con-

TOY BOX ON CASTERS

veniently sized box of playthings can be transported easily if you are going on a trip or a short visit.

Use open shelves to display toys. Every child has some toys that shouldn't be tossed haphazardly into a bin when not in use. And the child usually wants to

show them to anyone he can tow into his bedroom. Open shelving is one way of meeting this situation. Open shelves can be arrayed along one wall, or even mounted in a window. In either case, try to keep the shelves mostly low, with the top shelf no higher than the child can reach. But for mementos or meaningful gifts, you might want to place some shelves higher. In most cases, shelves 12 inches deep will be adequate, though you will probably want to build a few at least 24 inches deep for larger toys.

Store ongoing games so they are ready for use. Storing games-in-progress intact is timesaving, but you'll want them to be out of the way.

Slide-out trays or shallow drawers fitted into a cabinet about 15 inches deep will hold most board games. Another device is to have a mounted system swing up into a bookcase. Or attach a game to one side of a board which can be reversed. A fourth method is to hinge a box-shaped lid to a table. When the lid is set down over the game board, it can serve as another work surface. You can make use of ceiling space by pulling a game board up to the ceiling with sash cord and pulleys.

Adaptable work areas

A desk that grows with a child and adapts to changing interests is best.

Commercially built or built in? The work area is the one exception to the rule of avoiding built-ins for children's rooms. Your child's bedroom may be too small for available commercially built units, or the design of the room may be wrong. A

CHANGEABLE DESK SUPPORTS

built-in work surface might be the only answer. Or, if floor space is at a premium, consider a wall desk with a fold-out work surface.

Work surface materials must be sturdy enough to withstand the wear and tear that a child can give. Most hardwoods will wear a long time, but they can be marred, scratched, and gouged. A covering of laminated plastic can be the answer to these problems, depending on the sort of use it will receive.

Adjustable *closet rod rests in notches on sides of closet. Architect: Morgan Stedman.*

Built-in drawers *under window seat have full extension glides. Architect: George Cody.*

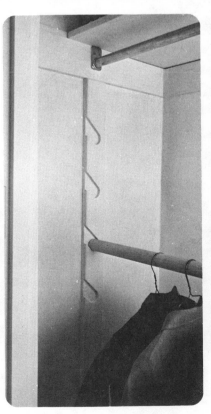

Fort under bunk *has boy-height entrance, peek hole at far left. Toy box, shelves are attached; steps are hardwood. Designer: Bill Pratt.*

Practical toy boxes

Fiber drums decorated with latex paint, wallpaper scraps, or self-adhesive vinyl hold teddy bears or baseball bats.

Divided in sections, counter top lifts to disclose shallow storage for toys. Bins below provide more storage, roll on casters.

Traveling box goes wherever its owner wants to do her coloring, holds toys too. Hardboard panels on top slide apart to form drawing table; sides have finger holes or handles; dividers separate supplies inside.

Two wood ladders fastened to the wall and ceiling support 1 by 6-foot-long boards between rungs. *Designer: John T. Jacobsen.*

Named boxes *on wide, adjustable shelves separate private property; complicated games stay on upper shelf, easy ones on lower. Centered paper holder and cutter supplies newsprint drawing paper. Table surface swings down; louvered doors close on whole cupboard.*

These desks adapt

Desk large enough for two *children raises on bolts as they grow. Drawer openings have plastic billfold flaps inside to keep out dust. Designer: Richard Lewis.*

Oversized art table *features top made from a single sheet of plywood, coated with clear sealer to protect from crayons, glue. Designer: Gordon Hammond.*

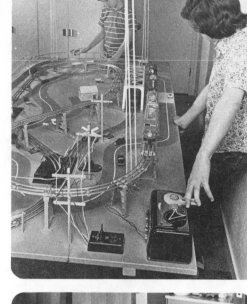

Ropes lower *this train board for use, raise it—with the aid of a winch—by means of pulleys on the board and rafters overhead.*

Putting away toys...why not make it easier?

Toy box trucks—*one for each child— drive out of tidy garage, transporting toys around family room. Architects: Lemmon, Freeth, Haines & Jones, Ltd.*

For now, *a preschooler's toy cabinet; later, with doors and shelves removed, a desk.*

Window seat *becomes ample bin for books and games when top lifts. Architect: Neal Lindstrom.*

Unusual storage combinations

Changeable closet's left side, fitted with removable storage unit, includes bins on casters. On right side, lowering the clothes rod gave extra shelf space. Doors, constructed with hardboard top sections, offer a bulletin board or a chalkboard on the lower half.

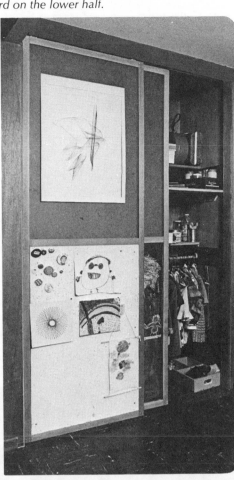

Lower the chained bunk to sleep a guest (the hinged hardwood strip below supports, steadies it); raise it to use as a blackboard.

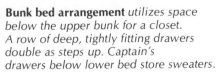

Bunk bed arrangement utilizes space below the upper bunk for a closet. A row of deep, tightly fitting drawers double as steps up. Captain's drawers below lower bed store sweaters.

In the Entry or Bedroom

The three general areas for clothes storage are the bedroom or dressing area, the hall closet, and closets for work clothes. Some families combine clothes storage with other general storage facilities in a room divider or storage wall. This preference can eliminate a separate hall or chore closet. Others like to keep different types of clothing apart.

Many homes are built with a central, shelved linen closet in the bedroom area. (See pages 66–73 for more information about storing linens and modifying a linen closet.)

A bedroom closet or a storage wall?

The bedroom with surplus closet space is a rarity. Consequently, you'll probably need to plan bedroom storage space in detail.

The storage units usually required in a bedroom or dressing area are: rods for hanging garments; drawers for folded clothes; specialized shelving for hats,

purses, and other accessories; a hamper for dirty clothes; and a rack or special closet for shoes. It used to be that these

LOWERED CLOSET FLOOR

storage units were separated: a wardrobe closet, one or two chests of drawers, a dressing table. But to save space and coordinate clothes storage, architects often combine all units into one—either an extended closet or a storage wall.

Standard closets should be at least 22 inches deep to allow enough room to hang clothes on a rod parallel with the door. If you're building a new closet, a steel wardrobe with cracks sealed by masking tape will protect clothing from moths.

A cedar lining can rejuvenate an old closet and keep your clothes safe from moths. Varnishing finishing cedar seals in the wood's fragrance. You can renew the aroma by sanding the wood lightly. Also, particle board made of aromatic red cedar flakes is sometimes available. Cedar repels moths but doesn't kill them, so wool clothes should be cleaned before they're stored.

A walk-in closet may be just what you need if you have the extra space for one.

Black and white paint *accents hinged doors of shelves and cabinets built into an upstairs hallway wall.*

Movable closet *with adjustable shelves, drawers lets owner rearrange space. Architect: Dartmond Cherk.*

A new walk-in usually requires extensive remodeling, possibly necessitating professional help. But, you will be rewarded with ample space for clothes rods on two

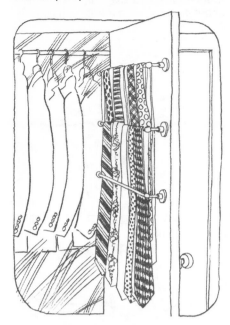

TIES ON TOWEL BARS

or three walls and plenty of area for drawers and shelving, plus the biggest advantage of a walk-in: easy access.

A storage wall usually covers or forms one entire wall of the bedroom. The standard depth requirement for this type of unit is about 24 inches. If you don't have quite that much space, installing a pull-out clothes rod on which clothes are hung parallel to the door might be your answer. The clothes rod is pulled into the room while you select garments—then returned to the closet when not in use. These easy-to-install metal rods are available to fit almost any size closet.

Many home builders conserve on space and materials by making one storage wall serve two rooms. These structures may or may not be load-bearing partitions. A wall of this type could be approximately 36 inches deep, with 24 inches on one side for the wardrobe and 12 inches on the other side for shelves and shoes.

When planning a storage wall, keep in mind that there is no "standard" organization. And remember to provide easy access to all the clothes.

Tailoring your closet

The interior of a closet or other clothing storage unit should be designed around your individual wardrobe. Of course, you will want to put every available inch of space to work. Commercial closet organizers of many sorts are available. Folding hanger holders, hanging shoe trees, and a plethora of tie holders line the shelves of hardware stores.

For hanging garments, group by length. This will provide uniform space beneath some of the groups to accommodate another clothes rod or space for drawers or shelves.

For folded garments, use shallow drawers or shelves. This will help prevent heavy piling and wrinkling. Drawers and sliding shelves are very useful for folded

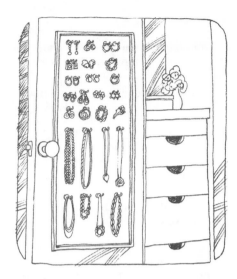

JEWELRY RACK

clothes. A 12-inch depth should be adequate, but depth and width depend primarily on how you fold the clothes.

(Continued on next page)

Bank of drawers *stores accessories and clothes; dividers separate purses. Architect: Herman Brookman.*

Disappearing vanity's top *pulls down, section above swings back. Wall unit includes adjustable shelves. Architect: Sidney Snyder.*

For shoes, fit pairs into a small area to take advantage of their uniformity of size. Even with a very narrow (10 or 12-inch) opening, 4 to 6 feet high and 12 inches deep, you can store six to eight pairs of shoes by using adjustable shelving. Actually, you can make shoes fit into almost any available space. A narrow opening between studs is deep enough for a hanging shoe bag; the slanted floor of a closet can accommodate several pairs; a rolling cart that slides under hanging clothes can keep shoes in order; commercially built racks inserted under hanging clothes keep shoes off the floor and easy to reach.

For hats and accessories, use open shelving. Hats, purses, and jewelry can be stored within easy reach by compartmentalizing an open section of wall into 12-inch squares. Seldom-used articles can be stored on shelves above hanging clothes or in a low drawer.

The double-purpose hall closet

A hall closet often both stores the coats, hats, and umbrellas of your family and provides temporary storage for the wraps of guests.

This closet can serve as a screen between the front door and living areas.

It can also be combined with a desk, music cabinets, or bookcase to form a complete free-standing storage wall.

Basic requirements are simple. A hall closet should be at least 24 inches deep and 24 inches wide. The clothes pole should be high enough to handle long coats. A shelf hung approximately 3 inches above the clothes rod for hats and accessories and a space below for boots and overshoes are very practical.

Closets for work clothes

A closet for storing chore clothes and outdoor garments might be just what you need. Sometimes a complete mud room, where you can change from heavy weather and work clothes, is desirable.

Hooks suffice for hanging up outdoor clothing, since there is really no need to keep work clothes neat and tidy on hangers. Using hooks reduces the amount of space needed. An area 16 to 20 inches deep, 4 feet wide, and 6 feet high will do the trick. However, if there are coats or shirts you want on hangers, place the hangers on the clothes hooks so the width of the piece of clothing is parallel to the door. The hooks should be placed at least 60 inches off the floor and 10 inches apart. If you decide to set a shelf above them, leave 3 to 4 inches of clearance space below the shelf to facilitate hanging garments on hooks.

A shelf or the floor can be used for shoes. If shoes need to dry out, a lath shelf about 4 inches off the floor will provide

ENTRY CLOSET

air circulation. To facilitate easy cleaning, the shelf can be set on cleats—it doesn't have to be nailed down.

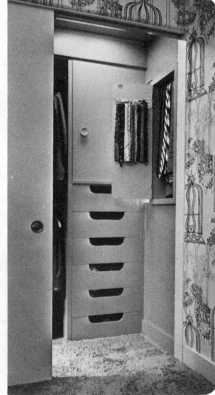

Closet wall for two people uses 2-foot recess between the doors and wardrobe inside as entry space. On one end, pull-out sectioned cabinet stores shoes; larger cabinet on other end contains shoe rack. Sweaters and other folded pieces fit inside shallow drawers. Ties hang on rack in side wall recess. Architect: Harold Gangnes.

Hinged panel *swings up to form table supported by gate leg brace, conceals blankets when closed. Another panel pulls out for headrest. Designer: Paul D. Jones.*

Bedside storage

Slanting headboard opens *for blanket, pillow storage; shelves above keep books within easy reach. Designer: Harold Sylvester.*

Boxes on all sides *frame bed, look like bolsters. Tops hinge open, revealing divided bins. Designer: Rick Morrall. (Also see front cover.)*

Modular boxes *of plywood stack inside closet. Shelves and drawer splines slide in slots spaced every 2 inches along sides of boxes.*

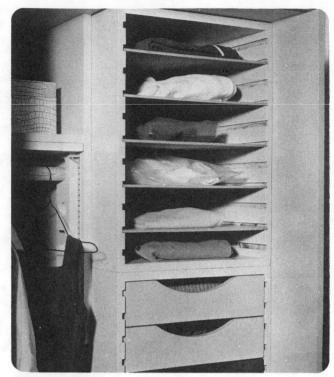

Fitting in accessories

Eggcrate partitions *divide drawer into sock-sized compartments. Row of dowels makes well-ventilated shoe rack. Architect: John Dinwiddie.*

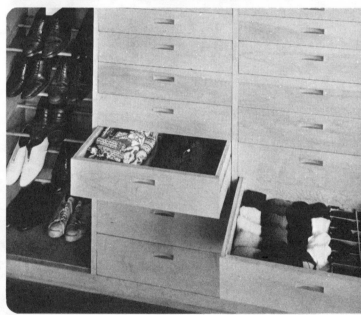

Hat cabinet *uses cut-out shelves to support wide brims. Other accessories fit on shelf space between, below hats.*

Clear plastic *small parts drawers— 32 of them in a built-in metal frame—hold jewelry collection. Designers: Lillis and Smith.*

Using closet space efficiently

Divided sections *hold sweaters, shirts; glass-fronted drawers pull out below. Architect: Bradford P. Shaw.*

Each stacked *clear plastic drawer holds a pair of shoes; metal clothes rod fits below.*

Dowel slack hangers *fit into drilled holes; short dowels hang beads and belts. Lipped hardboard shelves replace drawers. Hardboard sections forming shoe bins slide in saw kerfs in frame on door. Architect: George T. Johnson.*

Full-length mirror, *bench, good lighting, and carpeting turn walk-in closet into a dressing room. Built-in bureaus make use of the space underneath clothes rods. Architects: Fletcher & Finch.*

Closets for outdoor clothing

Family coat closet *uses space under stairway in entrance hall. Stack of open shelves on the right holds books, hats, purses, miscellany.*

Inside front door, *lighted and mirrored alcove includes rain gear bin with padded and carpeted lid.*

Space-saving clothes rack *next to the door has hat-coat hooks, shelf, mirror for a last-minute look. Architect: Marvin Witt, Jr.*

Heated, drip-dry closet *has a water seal at the floor edge. Warm air enters through furnace register at bottom, circulates up through clothes and out the louvered doors. Socks dry on a portable rack. Architect: Burr Richards.*

Movable storage unit *consists of frame of welded wire set out 2 inches from the back; bench with a shoe box under its hinged top. Architect: Marvin Witt, Jr.*

To camouflage this coatrack, *coat pegs become a part of the overall wall pattern when no coats are hanging. The pegs, also acting as spacers between boards, protrude a few inches outward. Architect: James A. Jennings.*

Triangular closet *fits precisely into space between front door and stairway. Sliding door hardware accents structure; plants cluster on deep shelf above. Designer: William K. Stout.*

In a Home Office, Hobby Room, or Sewing Room

Home offices, sewing centers, and hobby rooms have certain storage needs in common. Both sewing and office areas usually require a space for a fairly sizable machine (typewriter or sewing machine), a spread-out work surface, and compartmented, within-arm's-reach storage for a miscellany of tools and supplies. (See pages 88, 95 for storage ideas for home workshops.)

These rooms or parts of rooms tend to look cluttered because of ongoing projects and the convenience of open storage. So, ideally, they should be set up in an out-of-the-way location or a concealable space.

Use the location

The most important considerations in planning storage for a home office, sewing, or hobby center are: 1) location in relation to the rest of the house,

2) amount of storage space required or needed, and 3) convenience for the one who uses it most.

A closet 24 to 27 inches deep allows enough room for work space and base-cabinet storage. It should be at least 5 feet wide to be comfortable. A dressmaker's dummy added to a sewing closet will normally take up an 18-inch-square space.

The living room often has enough free wall space to add a desk or work area. However, providing storage units that blend in with the rest of the furnishings and decor in this room can be a problem. And keeping the work surface in order may be a frustrating experience, especially if you are interrupted by unexpected guests.

A den or family room can be a practical location for a work area and adjacent storage, depending on several factors,

including the number of children in the household, their ages and activities, and the location of the television set. If the family room is big enough, a desk might be placed at one end and the television at the other.

The bedroom is one location that usually can be closed off to provide a quiet place to work. However, it might also be a room that's already cramped for space. Here, as in the case of children's rooms, a built-in work surface might be the only answer. Or, a wall desk that can be folded down for use may provide enough work area.

The dining room offers one obvious advantage: a generous-sized work surface that's already in place. Also, most dining areas are traffic-free. One disadvantage is that you may have to store the typewriter, sewing machine, or other paraphernalia in another part of the

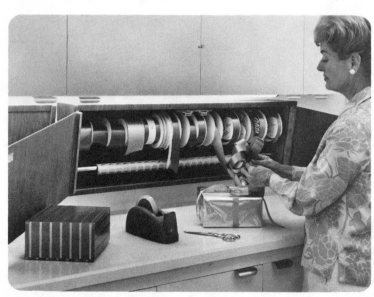

Ribbon and wrapping paper *hang on dowels in long, shallow cupboard above a countertop. Designer: Louis Mazzetti.*

Rearrange *some modular boxes, fit them with drawers and shelves, turn them to face a different way—whatever your office needs.*

house—unless there is a dining room cabinet or buffet with a spare drawer or two.

The kitchen is often overlooked for office use, and it may already contain a counter, small table, or space around the telephone where paperwork can be stored and worked at efficiently.

Easy-to-reach equipment

Your sewing, letter writing, or craft project will certainly progress more smoothly if the tools and supplies you need are close at hand. You can buy commercial units designed specifically for the items you store, or you can try your own improvisations.

Work surfaces form the center around which storage is arranged. Where space is really at a premium, a table top that folds back against a wall or into a cabinet might be an answer. Part of a work surface can tilt up from the horizontal to form a slanted drawing or writing board.

A workbench or table need not be built in. Why not consider using a solid or hollow-core door, a metal mess table (from a sporting goods store), or even a ping-pong table? Irregular doors from hardware and lumber stores won't work in a doorway, but they make fine inexpensive desk tops.

For a sit-down-height (29 to 31 inches) table, mount a table top on storage

TILT-UP DESK TOP

chests, kitchen base cabinets, or filing cabinets. For stand-up or tall stool-height tables (36 to 40 inches), the top can be mounted on high sawhorses or large storage units.

To conceal your work without having to put everything away, try variations on the roll-top desk idea. A tilt-down or fold-down (or up, or sideways) panel can be installed to fit over your work surface. Or, use a lift-off cover.

A sewing machine or typewriter can be mounted on a swing-out shelf, a movable cart, a pop-up or pull-out stand, or a sliding platform. Any of these will allow you work space and hidden storage, and will avoid the inconvenience of

lifting or carrying a bulky machine to point of use. If a machine is stored on top of the work surface, valuable working area is reduced.

An electric typewriter or an elaborate sewing machine requires more room than a standard model. Measure your machine to find the dimensions of the minimum space it will fit in. If the sew-

PULL-OUT SHELF

ing machine is kept on the work surface, allow a few extra inches of space behind it for moving fabric.

Most supplies and reference materials are best kept in filing cabinets, deep drawers, and wide, open shelves. A map cabinet is useful for storing large, flat items. For large sheets of heavy paper or canvases, vertical dividers work well.

Tightly grouped, *wide plywood drawers use lip as pull and horizontal reinforcer. Designer: Design Format.*

Panels drop down *to provide work surfaces for sewing and writing, with storage above and below.*

Wall secretary *adapts to size and number of pockets needed. Designer: Steve Smith.*

Start *with standard cardboard file boxes. Build a frame to fit their outside dimensions, cover front panels, add porcelain knobs to make an attractive file cabinet.*

Filing cabinets can be used for storing patterns or important papers. Cabinets are made of materials ranging from colorful cardboard to heavy-duty metal and come in many sizes—for legal-sized papers on down to 3-by-5-inch cards. Larger files require more space, of course, including enough space around the cabinet to pull out drawers and still leave room for you to move around easily.

Bolts of fabric, binders, reference books, and telephone books can be stored conveniently on open shelving. For this type of storage around the work surface, you can either make the bookshelves part of the desk or hang them independently on a facing wall. Either way, consider the possibility of converting a section of shelving to pigeonholes for miscellaneous supplies.

Small tools and implements can be fitted into a variety of storage containers. Pull-out shelves, shallow drawers, and

PARTITIONED DRAWER

narrow shelving are better than deep drawers for storing pointed instruments.

• *Small drawers* around a desk can be valuable for storing paper, ink pads, pencils, paper clips, and other small items. With clear plastic drawers, you can see what's inside. Molded plastic bins and tubs are colorful and inexpensive.

• *Partitioned drawers*, divided according to the items stored, avoid entangle-

ments and make it easier to put things back in the right place. Pull-out shelves can also be partitioned and fitted with narrow edgings to keep things from falling out. Drawers can be partitioned to the exact width of spools of thread, or spools can be mounted on dowels or rails set in a wall or on the back of a door. Commercially made spool and bobbin holders fit easily into a drawer and can be lifted out onto a counter.

• *A tackle box*, drawer parts cabinet, tool chest, or any smaller and lighter version of a machinist's tool chest will provide you with a variety of compartments.

• *Open storage* is probably the best system for small items that are used constantly. You can use pins, hooks, and racks to attach these items to a piece of perforated hardboard, corkboard, or bulletin board on a wall next to the sewing machine or desk.

Below the extra high *(39 inches) counter, open compartments handle most shapes and sizes of canvas. Perforated hardboard panel on end wall provides hanging space, temporary storage for paintings in progress.*

Large, shallow drawers *recessed into wall of sewing closet save working space. Architect: Vladimir Ossipoff.*

Built-in storage for compact workplaces

Shelves appear *when desk swings down out of wall cabinet; hinged leg supports sturdy work surface.*

Stowing the sewing

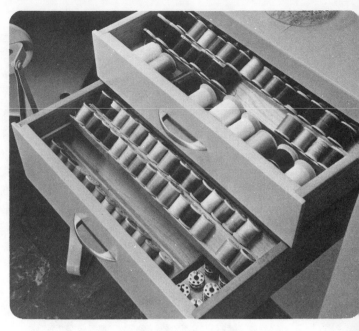

Spool drawers *use slanted, sliding trays; top drawer includes a special tray for larger spools. The nails hold bobbins but could be used for more spools.*

Hang *perforated hardboard panel as you would a picture; use narrow shelves, hardware hooks to organize tools.*

Rough-cut fencing, *tin baking pans, porcelain pulls make up wall-hung storage unit. Notches join the horizontal with vertical pieces. Designer: Rick Morrall.*

Shallow, pull-out drawers *behind cabinet doors contain fabrics, patterns. Sliding panels below window sill hide row of spools. Architect: Jerry Gropp.*

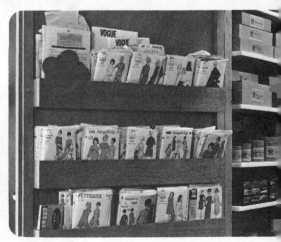

Wood-strip holders *attached to inside of closet door store patterns. Designer: William G. Shirreffs.*

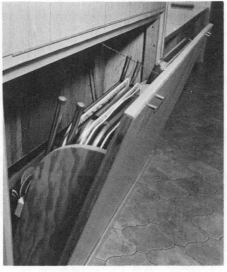

Combination storage wall *includes a drop-down board hinged along the bottom, resting on tilt-out section that holds cardtables, TV trays. Hinged cover conceals swing-up typewriter. Designer: Norman C. Loeber.*

Ideas for desk supplies

Two filing cabinets *face in opposite directions to form a divider/peninsula. Architect: James A. Jennings.*

Built-in desk *has shelves of assorted heights, bright plastic bins on wood runners. Architect: William Logan.*

Burners, *metal files, refrigerator, cabinets combine in office/guest room. Architect: Robert E. Small.*

Rolled drawings, *paper store neatly on door-mounted rack inside this closet. Designer: Judy Friedman; Architect: Raymond L. Lloyd.*

Hinged top *forms counter; series of narrow drawers organize paints. Designer: Ned Doll.*

Storing art...

Taborets *(rolling cabinets) on casters hold a variety of art supplies. They pull up next to a desk or function as work island in the center of a room.*

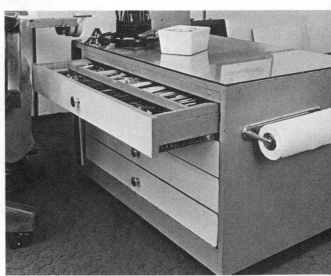

Slatted, partitioned *shelves over heated rods in closet with louvered doors provide mildew-free storage for paintings. Architect: Jerry Auld.*

Yarn bobbin rack, *suspended from beam, divides family room and studio. Row of hooded spotlights illuminates the colorful yarn. Architects: Liddle & Jones.*

...craft work, or hobby gear

Assortment of drawers, *open shelves, cabinets closed by sliding doors provides ample storage for sculpture tools, supplies. Architect: Perry Johanson.*

Paintings need slots *that hold them in a fairly upright position, easy to slide in and out. Here, a series of tall, deep slots complete a cabinet with shelves in front. On the door, softboard serves as pin-up surface.*

In a Linen Closet, Cleaning Closet, or Laundry

When washing meant tubs and washboards and clotheslines and sheer back-breaking labor, there was little choice as to where you put the laundry. It had to go in the utility room next to the back porch or in the basement. Today, although most people prefer to have a separate utility room, most medium-sized homes just don't have the necessary square footage. What do you do if this is the case in your home? Fortunately, the washer and dryer and accompanying storage can go anywhere in the house if you can provide them with the proper wiring and plumbing. Some portable washers and dryers don't require permanent installation, special plumbing, wiring, or venting.

In one large utility room, you might set up the washing machine and dryer, store bed and bath linens, and collect cleaning supplies. Or you can utilize separate alcoves or closets for each of these purposes. A laundry or utility room is sometimes also used as a mud room (see pages 52, 56–57).

Planning for the laundry, for your cleaning supplies, and for bed and bath linens is tied to the floor plan of your house—especially placement of the bedrooms and bathrooms—and to your housework patterns.

The complete laundry

Wherever the laundry is done, it is to your advantage to have additional space around the washer and dryer to allow for conveniences that help to make the laundry process run smoothly. A sink for scrubbing grease and stains, shelves for soaps and bleaches, and a place for an ironing board and iron all add efficiency.

Floor planning should begin with the washer and dryer because 1) plumbing requirements may limit the number of possible locations, and 2) because these appliances should be properly inter-related if work and storage efficiency are to be maximized. Remember to allow accessibility for repairs and easy cleanup if overflow should occur.

In arranging a laundry, remember that noise may be a problem, venting for heat and moisture may be difficult, and accumulation of odors from bleaches and other cleaning agents can be objectionable.

Minimum needs include a shelf or small cabinet for detergents and bleaches and a wastebasket for empty containers and lint. The more counter space you provide in a laundry, the better. Counter and shelves should be surfaced with a mate-

Lift off countertop section to use sink, fit back in place over sink to form flush counter surface. Designer: William K. Stout.

Mobile cleaning cart rolls on casters to other parts of house, stores in closet sized to fit. Architects: Akiyama, Kekoolani and Associates.

rial that's easy to keep clean and resistant to the corrosive action of laundry products such as bleach. You can put cabinets, bins, and shelves under the counter and more cabinets or shelves on the wall above the counter for storage.

Simple accessories that make good sense include a hand towel or a roll of paper towels hung beside the sink and adjustable shelves in the surrounding cabinets.

A place for drip-drys eliminates a line over the bathtub or shower. Because a drip-dry area requires a drain, it's usually best to provide for this area during building or remodeling. A folding clothes drying rack, for air-drying, is handy.

Ironing needs such as an ironing board, sprinkling bottle and starch, stool or chair, shelf for stacking ironed clothes and a rod for hanging clothes in the laundry room will save you steps. If you build an ironing board cabinet, check the board's measurements before you begin nailing and add a few inches to those figures for ease in removing and replacing it.

A laundry sorter, which is simply a divided bin, basket, or tub for organizing clothes into different machine loads as they are collected, can be built into a small cabinet.

Roll-around bins and drop-down bins, simple innovations for collecting clothes from the bedroom area, can save a great

ROLL-AROUND HAMPER

deal of work. Roll-around bins can be kept in bedrooms or bathrooms part of the time as laundry hampers, then wheeled into a utility room.

A mending center with space for a sewing machine plus accessories (see pages 58–63) enables you to repair clothes as they come from the dryer. Pull-out trays for scissors, spools of thread, and pins and needles take hardly any space. Place the sewing machine where you can sew

and launder simultaneously, if the noise doesn't bother you.

An indoor gardening center in the laundry room is a possibility if you have counter space and a sink. Simply reserve one cabinet for potting materials and containers, and you'll be able to tend to your house plants between laundry chores.

Linen storage

Storing linens will be faster and easier if you have a place to fold and sort them. Ideally this is in the laundry room, where you can fold sheets and towels while they're still warm and unwrinkled from the dryer. If you don't have space in the laundry area, you might install a counter top or drop-down or fold-out table in or next to a linen closet.

Many of the same principles used in detailing table linen storage (see pages 26–31) can be applied to storing bed and bath linens. Usually the most convenient place to store bed and bath linens is between the bedroom area and the laundry.

A pass-through cabinet is the best way to link the laundry and bedrooms. The linens can be sorted, folded, and stored as they come from the dryer. As it is needed, each piece can be removed

Blankets *hang on holders that slide on waxed cabinet floor. Flat pieces fit above.*

Board pulls out *to hold linen for folding and sorting; double doors close off shelves. Architect: Ralph Anderson.*

Tangerine-and-white *hanging panels of duck hide clothes hamper and ironing board.*

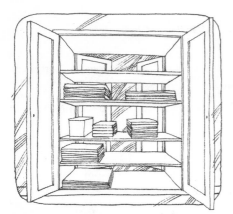

PASS-THROUGH CABINET

through the opposite side of the cabinet or closet. Some pass-through units include clothes bins which can be opened in the bedroom or bath for loading and then emptied in the laundry.

Shelves above the washer and dryer can serve as additional linen storage space. There may also be space beside the appliances for bins or drawers for storing laundry and cleaning supplies.

The cleaning closet

A single storage closet for the cleaning implements you use throughout the house can save time and trouble in the never-ending process of keeping a house in order. A favorite spot for centralized cleaning equipment storage is a closet in a hallway.

Closet design depends on what's kept inside. The wide range of shapes and sizes of cleaning items to be stored—brooms, mops, vacuum cleaner, dustpans, window washing equipment, waxes, soaps, disinfectants, buckets—points up the difficulty of designing a single closet for these tools. But there are prefabricated units available which will

provide adequate storage for most houses. Cleaning closet dimensions of 16 to 20 inches deep, at least 65 inches high, and at least 24 inches wide (though width can be variable) will form an adequate space. You can hang implements on the walls, use the back of the closet door to store long attachments, and install shelves for small items. Shelves

CLEANING CLOSET

shouldn't be so deep that supplies disappear or can be knocked over. Alternate handle-up and handle-down mops and brooms to fit more in. Let air circulate around oily cleaning cloths to prevent spontaneous combustion.

Specialized closets for particular rooms should be kept within those rooms. The bathroom and kitchen, for example, have specialized cleaning problems for which you should keep particular tools and supplies on hand. A cabinet, space under the sink, an unused drawer, or part of a closet can be made into a compact cleaning supply center.

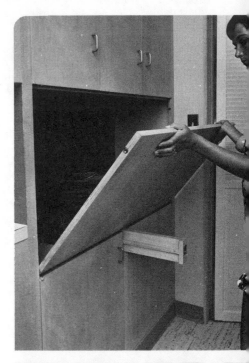

Laundry-sewing room has work counter, storage cupboard with fold-down front that becomes a cutting board or table for folding clothes. Single center support pulls out from between cabinets. Architect: Donald D. Chapman.

Cleaning implements *share closet with ironing board and iron. Designer: Norman V. Manoogian.*

Full-sized *ironing board pivots out of slot under counter. Movable bin holds unironed clothes; drawers store linens. Architect: William J. Bain, Jr.*

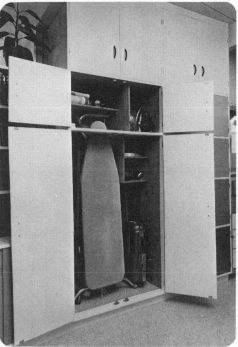

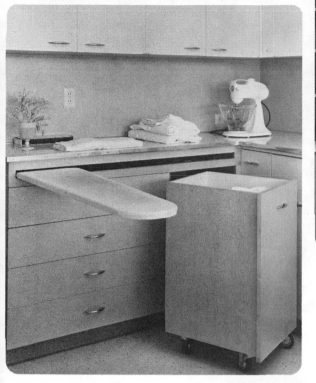

Built-in ironing cupboard *with board and outlet fits into wall at open end of a U-shaped kitchen. Designer: Dallas E. Zeiger.*

Here's how to make room for an ironing board

Ironing board *stores in this cupboard along with fold-up, felt-covered cutting table; irons on small shelves. Architect: William A. Patrick.*

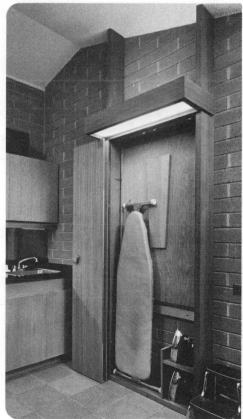

Cupboard within a cupboard *holds cleaning supplies on both sets of doors. Architects: Hughan & Hughan.*

Between-levels closet, *beside the stairway landing, saves steps in a two-story house. Folding doors conceal it. Designer: Halsey Jones.*

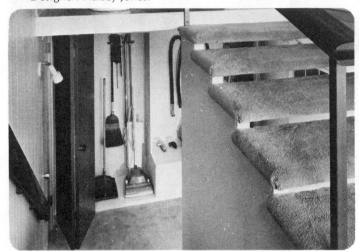

Arranging a closet for cleaning supplies

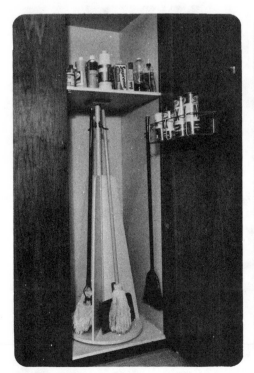

Revolving stand *for brooms takes up small space in this closet, allows shelf above. Designer: Fred Blair Green.*

Perforated hardboard *lines side and back of closet; tools hang on individual hooks. Shelves line the left wall.*

Two long, high *shelves accommodate bottles, cans; mops and brooms hang below. Architect: John McGough.*

From closet to laundry

Headed for washing machine, *linens, clothing pass through wall from master bath to laundry via these long drawers. Perforated hardboard ventilates drawer bottoms, a door.*

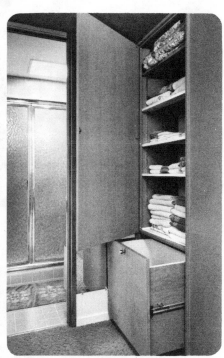

Tilt-out bin *addition to linen closet stores linens, clothing ready for washing. Architect: Paul Hayden Kirk.*

Slide-out laundry drawer *in dressing area conceals soiled towels; fresh linens above. Architect: Edward Sullam.*

Two-way closet *between laundry room and bedroom hallway looks like conventional closet from hall. In laundry, drop-down hinged panel serves as counter for folding clothes; chains support it. Designer: Jan Currey.*

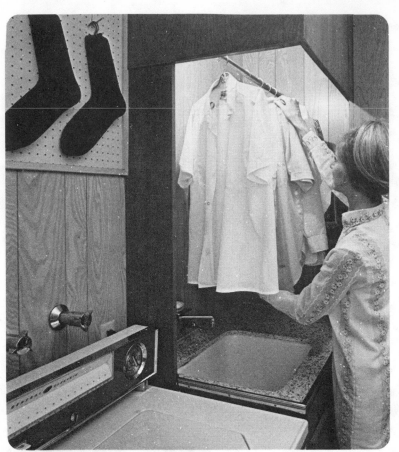

Storage above, around, or next to the washer & dryer

Drying cabinet, *open on two sides for air circulation and access, includes a rod for hanging clothes and a ceiling vent fan used in damp weather. Counter top below slants down on all four sides so dripping water drains into the laundry basin.*

Mending supplies *fit into drawers. Architects: Allan & Olsson.*

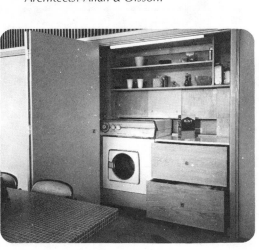

Handsome cabinetry *houses washer, dryer in family-and-dining room. Upper section hangs on wall; lower part pulls out. Designer: W. Verne Stevenson.*

Laundry closet *includes deep roll-out drawers, counter space for sorting, shelves, and cabinets behind sliding panels. Folding doors conceal the area when not in use. Architect: Alfred Preis.*

To simplify laundry sorting...

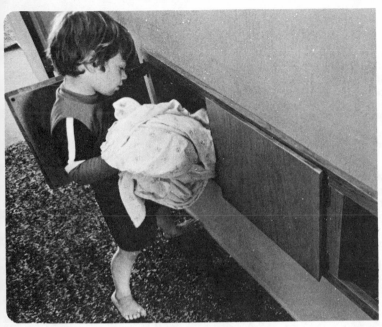 

Labor saving super-hamper (and laundry sorter) built in between laundry room and adjoining hallway consists of three labeled, separate bins: for perma press, color, and white. Designer: Patricia C. Lum.

Eye-level bins above washer, dryer keep loads separate; perforations in bottom of bins promote air circulation. Architects: Bain and Overturf.

In the Bathroom

The amount of bathroom storage you need depends in part on the storage arrangements in other rooms. For example, if your hall closet is adequate for storing linens (see pages 67–73), and cleaning supplies (see pages 68–73) are stored in a central cleaning closet, then a bathroom medicine cabinet and perhaps a clothes hamper or bin will meet your needs. But, more storage space in a bathroom can help relieve overcrowded conditions in other parts of the house.

In a new bathroom

While you're still in the planning stage, list the articles for which bathroom space is required—even if they're used for just a few minutes each day. Separate these items into categories: those that can be kept within view, small items, large things requiring a big storage space, items that need to be locked up. Then estimate the amount of space needed to hold whatever's in each category.

Recessed cabinets and shelves for a new house can be quite large. If you're remodeling an existing bathroom, however, installing larger or additional recessed storage will be more difficult because of in-place studs, pipes, and electric cables (which are expensive to move).

Surface-mounted cabinets and shelves are less liable to transmit sound through walls than recessed cabinets, but they are also more obtrusive. If the front of a surface-mounted cabinet is mirrored, it can be difficult to light it properly.

Visible storage (see page 4) can be used in bathrooms just as in other parts of the house. Use walls and cabinet doors for rods, hooks, and various types of shelving.

Reusing existing space

If you plan to remodel a bathroom, it makes sense to consider including some built-in storage. But there are several possibilities for adding cabinets and closets in the bathroom without remodeling and without reducing the amount of floor space.

Replace old cabinets with modern versions designed to hang on a wall or fit between the studs. Often, two or three cabinets hung to fill a wall will accommodate all the tubes, jars, and bottles that collect on counters and window sills.

A hint to remember if you decide to build your own medicine cabinet: set the shelves 4 to 6 inches apart, with at least one shelf 9 inches high to accommodate taller bottles.

Utilize a section of open wall, such as the area between the medicine cabinet and the ceiling, space over the toilet, and square footage above the bathtub. Shelves and cabinets need only be 8 to 10 inches deep to hold bath towels and other supplies. If they are fitted between the studs, they will project into the room only 4 to 6 inches.

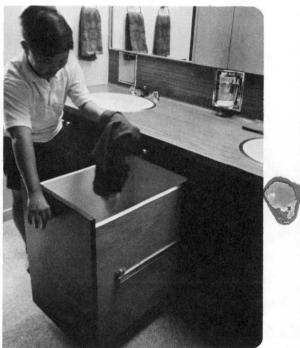

Recessed tumbler and toothbrush holders swing out from behind chrome panels. Clothes hamper fits beneath counter. Architect: Edward Sullam.

Enclose space beneath the sink with a free-standing or built-in cabinet. This can be a simple box with a slot cut in the

COMBINATION STORAGE WALL

back to allow for the drainpipe. Remember to leave some working room in case the plumbing needs repair. This enclosure (or complete cabinet) should be a foot or more wider than the basin to be

useful—otherwise the plumbing takes up too great a proportion of space. Shelves or hooks can be attached to the cabinet sides and doors.

Adding accessories

Many commercial items are available to save space and add convenience, and most are quite easy to install. Or you can build your own accessories out of wood, metal, or plastic.

Towel bars, rings, and ladders can be combined for different effects. One 36-inch towel bar for each user of the bathroom is usually enough. Swinging towel bars save space; or you can construct a towel ladder with as many rungs as you like. Towel rings are useful for storing extra towels, but towels dry faster when draped over a bar.

Space around fixtures can be used to good effect; for example, you can place a small shelf for bottles above a shower head. A pole shelf placed against a wall, supported by floor-to-ceiling braces, is another space saver. These units come with interchangeable and adjustable shelves. Other conveniences you might consider include two-roll paper holders, dispensers for facial tissues that can be attached to a wall, and a combination toothbrush, tumbler, and soap rack that revolves into a wall recess.

TOWEL LADDER

Accessories in children's baths make them more usable. If you have small children, the bottom drawer of a vanity cabinet can be fitted with a solid top and used as a retractable step for reaching the basin. A special cabinet just for a child might encourage keeping bath toys and supplies orderly.

Hand towels, *face towels make easy to reach, decorative display. You could adjust sizes, shapes of spaces for toiletries or towels. Designer: Sabin O'Neal.*

Planter *at end of tub adds storage space for toiletries and cosmetics. Designer: J. R. Davidson.*

Combination *of shelves behind door, drawers, and a roll-out bin store towels and clothing in bath. Architect: George Cody; Interior Designer: Stewart Morton.*

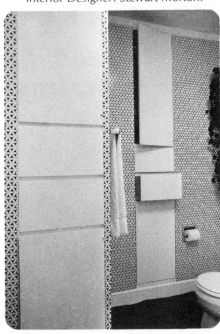

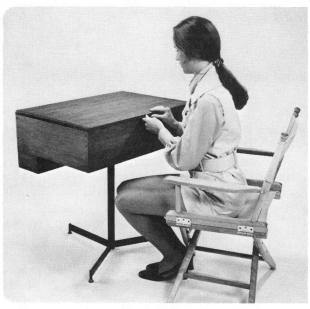

Make-up table *looks like an old school desk, conceals collection of bottles and brushes while leaving top clear. Commercial metal base supports box with removable insert; light bulbs flank mirror. Designer: Peter Whiteley.*

Organizing grooming extras

Shoe buffer, *plugged into wall socket and set on a sliding shelf, pulls out of cabinet when needed.*

Adding shelves *and towel rack around fixtures resulted in new look, more storage space without changes in walls or fixtures.*

Convenient clean towels

Cedar-lined closet *stores towels in slide-out trays; shelves adjust. Architects: Rushmore and Woodman.*

Floor-to-ceiling storage

Series *of drawers in varying heights forms tall partition between shower and the tub. Architect: Lloyd Ruocco.*

Between-the-studs *space contains storage cabinets. Towel hangers function as door pulls; scale tips out of bottom compartment. Architect: Anne Rysdale.*

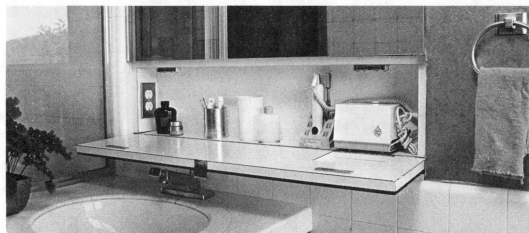

Mirror-covered door *swings down 90° on piano hinge, closes with magnetic catches. Recessed cabinet, one wall stud deep, has plastic laminate lining, electric outlets at both ends. Architects: Wagstaff & McDonald.*

Childproof medicine cabinet *locks with flush, loose-fitting metal pin (or nail) dropped through hole into door. Small magnet pulls the pin up. Adding the plywood door transformed hall linen closet shelf into generous cabinet.*

ordinary medicine cabinet

Hidden shelves behind pegboard panel placed conveniently above a bathtub store miscellany. Architect: Vladimir Ossipoff.

Just four shelves attached to a wall, simple cabinet has L-shaped door with mitered corners, no catch. Architect: Frank S. Robert.

Rosewood pieces of varying sizes glued on a plywood panel cover small cabinet, create interesting texture. Designer: John Kapel.

Steplike plywood arrangement sized to fit existing drawer holds bottles and jars at an angle, making cosmetic and prescription labels easy to read.

In an Attic or Basement

Both attics and basements must be reasonably easy to reach to be practical for storage. And if they're unfinished, the items you store must be protected from extremes—of heat and cold in the attic and of moisture in the basement.

Even if your attic or basement is unfinished and rarely used, it should be orderly enough so that you can find what you're looking for easily. But other than a basic system of organization, attic and basement storage generally requires less neatness, ingenuity, and expense than storage in the rest of the house.

See the chapter on garden and garage storage (pages 86–95) for storage ideas that might be transferable to an attic or basement.

Under the rafters

Many attics weren't built for storage, so find out how much weight your attic floor will bear before stacking up heavy items. If your attic has a catwalk only, lay pieces of plywood across the structure to make a usable surface. If you're storing

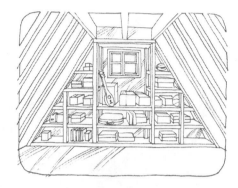

GABLE END SHELVING

things that are fragile, you might want to insulate the roof or add a ventilation fan as protection from temperature fluctuations.

Access. If your house is one with a ceiling hatch and fold-down ladder arrangement, carrying things to and from the attic is probably difficult and awkward. Some types of folding stairs are sturdier than others, though, and you can enlarge the hatch opening. A door-sized entrance with a permanent ladder or stairway is a much safer and easier way to reach an attic and will increase the attic's usefulness for storage.

Organization. In general, if your attic is sizable and used entirely for storage, you should arrange articles around the walls so all are in view and easy to reach. You can suspend rods across the rafters to hang garment bags; cover gable end walls with shelves; and use large triangular racks or specially shaped chests tucked under a sloping ceiling. Take advantage of a high roofline by driving nails or hooks into the rafters and then hanging garment bags, sports equipment, and other objects from the highest points.

Loft made into a library *uses shelves along walls and long, shallow drawers to take advantage of the structure for storage. Architect: Robert York.*

Shallow storage closets *for out-of-season clothes, slides, games run along side walls. Designer: Jerry Lamb.*

To keep track of what you're storing in your attic, group related objects together even if they're different sizes and shapes; label things that are concealed; and keep an inventory list. Protect furniture by surrounding it with mattress pads, and keep dust away by covering the furniture with plywood or hardboard or by draping it with plastic, paper, or fabric. You might cover shelves with carpet scraps to protect luggage and other heavy items from scrapes.

In the basement

Dampness, in the form of humidity, condensation, and leaks, is the main drawback to using a basement for storage. But if you can solve the moisture problem, you'll find that the even temperature and manageable stairway in most basements make them ideal for certain types of storage.

Moisture protection is best accomplished by waterproofing the basement completely, inside and out. But if you're living with a damp basement and don't want to tackle the structural problems of waterproofing, you might still be able to use the space for storage. Choose metal storage units over wood—metal won't swell and stick, though it will corrode if the finish is scratched. Rubber or vinyl

weather stripping around the edges of basement doors and windows will help keep out moisture.

Leave room for air to circulate around fabric, such as clothing kept in a basement closet. Or suspend a rod between exposed pipes and hang garment bags from that. Closets should be raised about 4 inches off the floor and furred out from the foundation wall at least 1 inch. You can spread heavy sheet plastic between the floor of a closet and the concrete basement floor for further protection against dampness.

Attaching storage shelves or cabinets to basement walls can be accomplished in several ways. You can drill a hole in the concrete with a carbide-tipped bit, tap in a lead anchor or fiber anchor, and then drive a screw or bolt in; or you can use a hammer-activated stud driver to drive special nails or threaded metal studs into concrete. If your walls are concrete block, drill into the hollow space between the blocks and use split-wing toggle bolts.

If the ceiling is low, try nailing wide boards to the base of joists to form shelves for rarely used items.

Root cellars in older houses don't have dirt floors just because they were cheap and easy to construct. By helping to keep food cool and moist, these dirt floors

make the cellars excellent food storage areas. Root cellars usually have an outside entrance or windows that can be opened to ventilate and regulate the temperature inside. Many have insulat-

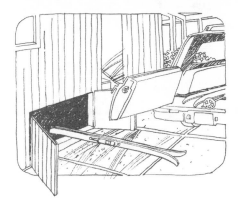

TRAPDOOR TO BASEMENT

ing material on the ceiling to prevent cold air in the cellar from chilling the whole house. Centrally heated homes with concrete floor basements are generally too warm to be used just as they are for food storage. But, part of almost any basement can be converted into a food storage room. See books on preserving foods for specific directions on setting up a root cellar.

Door to overhead storage *space pulls down with cord; spring holds it shut. Commercial ladder folds out in three sections, has some bounce at hinges but works well for reaching items needed seldom or seasonally.*

Curtains hide *clothes-storage shelves built against low, outward-sloping wall. Architect: David Tucker.*

Putting attic space to work

Openings cut in shaft *for a skylight that illuminates the stairwell beneath the attic floor allow light to escape out into the attic, eliminating the need for electric wiring. (Also see page 85.)*

Suspended from beams, *bookcases conform to roof pitch and utilize awkward space. Chains and 1 by 3s provide support. Designer: R. L. Loveless.*

Corner of basement includes wine rack, deep shelving, tall space for golf bag and skis. Opening to crawl space, next to wine rack, circulates cool air year-round.

Wedged-together shelves fit into the end of a hallway, a closet—any tall, narrow space. Glued to shelves, ¼ rounds keep them in place; side pieces act as spacers.

Try these ideas in the basement

Basement wine cellar, reached via a hatchway and ladder, stores wine in three different types of racks. Textured floor looks rustic, insulates.

Gaining access to the attic

Tower of stacking boxes *provides both access to storage loft and spiral display compartments. Plywood boxes based on a 1-foot-square module vary in size and shape. Architect: Dan Koberg.*

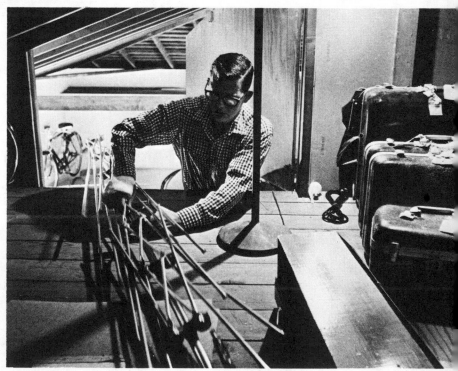

Rungs attached solidly *to workshop tool-storage panel (see page 95) in an attached garage provide footholds for climb into attic space of house. Luggage and sports gear load into car quickly from this attic access point; door swings shut to close off entrance to attic from the garage side.*

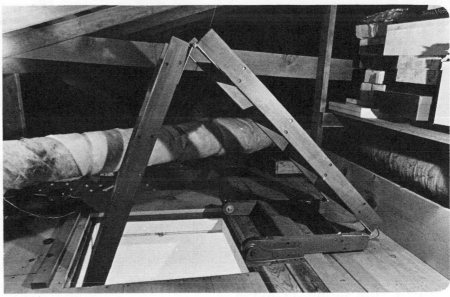

Hook pole unlatches door, *guides down three-section hinged ladder from a low-clearance attic. Built specifically for this location, the ladder fits into the original small attic opening. Designer: Norm Loeber.*

Removing section *of ceiling in large closet created both convenient entrance to attic and loft space. Ladders lead to carpeted loft, then to removable skylight and roof; door opens to spacious attic. Second skylight passes through center of attic (see page 82). Designer: Tom Plemons.*

Camouflaged door-mounted ladder *to attic doubles as a towel rack. Translucent overhead panel lifts off. Architect: Richard Ehrenberger.*

In the Garden or Garage

Many of the storage ideas in the preceding chapter on attics and basements (pages 80–85) cover some of the same equipment you can store in the garage or in the garden. But the easy indoor-outdoor access of storage in the garden and garage makes these places especially worth considering for garden supplies, tools, and sports equipment.

Garden work-storage centers

Though used primarily to keep equipment and supplies close to where you're working, a garden shelter can also prove useful as a screen—or fit into a narrow area that's unusable otherwise—or become a part of an already existing outdoor structure.

Check with codes and ordinances before you begin construction of a storage unit or position a prefabricated shelter. Some local building codes and zoning ordinances specify exactly how close to a side or backyard fence these structures can be placed. In many locations you can put a shed anywhere you want as long as it isn't anchored to the ground or on a concrete slab.

Location of a garden storage center will probably be determined by the size and shape of your lot. "The garden" is quite often two gardens (front and back) or even four gardens if you grow flowers or vegetables along the sides of your house. If you have a choice of where to store garden equipment and can't make up your mind, remember that it is a real advantage to have the storage area close to a driveway.

A generally workable plan is to locate the garden storage center at the side of the house and not too far from the garage. Other possible locations are against a back fence, adjacent to the patio, next to the garage, or in a back corner of your lot. In the latter case, the storage unit could be hidden by a simple fence or shrubbery.

An obvious solution that's often overlooked: have *two* garden storage locations, one (in the garage) for bulky or seldom-used items, the other (wherever most convenient) for items used more frequently.

Attached shelters can be either extensions of the present structure or self-contained units. You may be able to shorten a patio 3 or 4 feet and build a storage wall alongside the house. Another solution is to build a shed adjacent to the garage. Whatever choice is right for you, be sure to meet the basic requirements of 1) weatherproofing the unit, constructing a raised foundation, and finishing it on the exterior so that it blends harmoniously with the main house and its surroundings; and 2) designing for the future as well as the present, making the storage shed large enough to handle bulky items you plan to acquire and trying to anticipate which of your present inventory may be expendable in a few years.

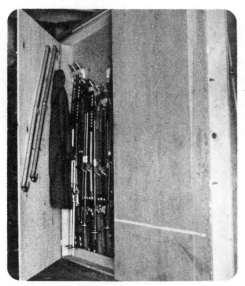

Closed, *ski cabinet (see back cover) leaves plenty of space for cars. Each pair of skis slides into blocks of wood securing bases and tips.*

Nailed to a wall, *combination of simple modular boxes makes handy garden storage and work center. Tops of boxes supply convenient counter surface.*

Drying tree *next to a swimming pool has a dowel trunk, dowel branches of varying lengths with wooden knob ends. Landscape Architect: Edward A. Damits.*

For an attached shed, you usually need a building permit and are limited by the plan and design of your house. You might have an architect or designer do the exterior, then plan the interior arrangements yourself. You could add a

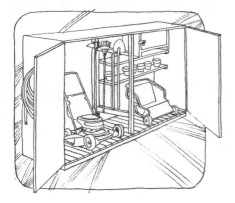

GARDEN SHELTER

connecting door to the house if you're building a full-sized shed, and you should have at least one window for light.

Detached sheds can be easier to build than attached shelters but are subject to more zoning and building code restrictions. Your local zoning or title restrictions might prohibit or limit erection of an outbuilding, or restrict running electricity or water to detached buildings. You can build your own detached storage shed, buy a prefab, or have one designed and built for you.

Prefabricated units are available in varying sizes and shapes. They provide adequate shelter for tools and supplies, but the interiors are not always equipped with drawers and bins or with devices for keeping hand tools separate from power tools. You may prefer to purchase the outside shell and design and build the interior according to your needs. With a wooden prefab you can usually line the inside walls with shelves, cabinets, etc.; a metal structure might have special provision for interior hangers.

It's best to set a prefab on a concrete slab because plywood or composition floors will wear out and frost and wind can cause movement of the shed. You need at least one window for light and ventilation. Prefabricated cabanas for swimming pools are usually not designed for storage.

Organizing a garage

The garage usually tends to become a catch-all for everything that's too bulky to be stored in the house. To prevent this from happening, try to consolidate every square inch of space not needed for cars and appliances. You may be surprised to find that you have one complete wall open for storage.

Use one wall to fit your individual needs. You may want one section filled with sturdy shelving for canned fruit, paint cans, or other small items. A second part may be left completely open for storage of bicycles, camping equipment, or lawn furniture. A third area can be a combination of shelving and an open space to hold a croquet set, golf clubs, or small boxes.

Plan door openings to admit the biggest things you will be storing or working on. You could make a combination partition/door to a storage area with 4-by-8-foot panels made into doors by adding hinges and hanging the panels on three or four strategically placed posts.

Look above the cars for more usable space. Whatever area is open above the cars is yours for the taking, but you must allow room for the garage door if it's the kind that slides overhead on a track or swings up.

Shelves suspended from the ceiling beams in the space above the car hood can often provide the amount of storage required.

Another way of using overhead space is a shelf operated by pulleys. The shelf is positioned on the garage floor and then lifted by supporting ropes run through pulleys. This method should be used only with relatively light objects that can be lifted easily. For stronger

Service wall *that takes advantage of an abrupt change in grade incorporates wood storage, sunken garbage cans, dairy and package delivery. (See additional views at right.) Architects: Kirk, Wallace, McKinley & Associates.*

Other side of two-story service wall *shows covered bin for wood – a half-cord fills bin up to driveway level. Delivery man opens gate from driveway, leaves food, packages, laundry in enclosed shelf just a few steps away from the kitchen-breakfast area.*

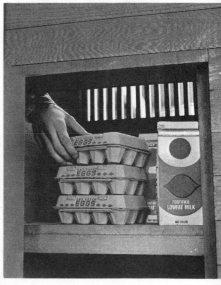

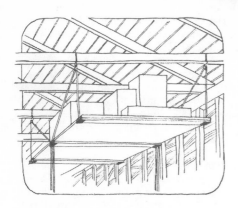

OVERHEAD PLATFORM

support, use 1-inch-wide iron straps bent 3 inches under the shelf and screwed to the bottom and sides. Attach a cable to the ends of the straps.

Utilizing a carport

A carport has almost as much available storage space as a garage. Because it's open, though, things must be kept neater and valuables must be locked up. You could install a closet extending the length or width of the carport—if the closet is 7 feet high and 3 feet deep it will hold garden furniture and other bulky items. The closet floor should be about 4 inches above the level of the carport floor to keep out water, so you might want a ramp to move heavy tools such as lawn mowers in and out.

Setting up a workshop

An unorganized workshop can leave you with damaged tools. By storing your tools carefully, so it's easy to locate the one you want, your projects will progress more smoothly.

Lumber can be stored on ladder racks similar to those used in lumberyards or on U-shaped racks placed below the ceiling joists. Plywood, gypsum wall-board, and other sheet materials can sag, twist, and warp, so stand them length-wise and cinch them snugly to a wall. Metal shelf brackets attached to wall studs will hold light pieces of lumber; space between the studs for vertical stacking is another easy solution, with simple crossbars to hold smaller pieces in place. A simple box in a dead corner will hold small scraps of lumber. If it has a lid, the closed box can serve as a temporary counter.

Small hand tools on open shelves or hooks are within easy reach; but if they're behind doors they stay cleaner and are safer. Placement of tools should be determined by frequency of use. The cheapest method for hanging tools is on nails of assorted sizes, or they can be hung on pegboard or spring clips. With a shallow cabinet, you can hang your tools on the back panel and on both sides of the doors. Two or more tool boards hung on a closet-door track in front of a stationary tool board is still another alternative.

Large power tools can be mounted on a movable bench (on locking casters) or stand that is big enough to accommodate large pieces of lumber. Attachments can be hung on the sides of the stand, and drawers and shelving can be fitted underneath.

Nails, nuts, and bolts are often corralled into glass jars and tin cans. You can keep small containers on simple shelves between the studs, edged with a strip of molding. Along the same line, you can save space by having one set of jars on top of a shelf and nailing the lids of another set to the underside of the shelf. Drawers separated with dividers, especially clear plastic ones, are also efficient for organizing small supplies.

Item-by-item storage

When planning storage for garden implements, sports equipment, and the other items you keep in a garden shelter or garage, allow for easy access. Keep sills low to avoid problems in moving wheeled implements. Also, make doors wide enough (about 5 feet) to clear the broadest lawn mower or tricycle.

Long-handled implements—such as rakes and hoes—can be hung vertically or horizontally in a storage unit 6 feet high and 6 feet wide. Hooks or brackets do the job, leaving the floor area clear for bulky implements, sacks, and boxes.

Loose garden materials such as fertilizers and soil-mixing ingredients (peat moss, leaf mold, etc.) can be stored in their bags in enclosed cabinets or boxes to keep moisture out. Use metal containers

CAN ON RACK

to protect edibles such as seed and bird feed; soil, sand, and vermiculite can be kept in open wooden boxes.

• *A garbage can* of plastic or metal can be mounted on a rack so material is easily shoveled out without moving the can. Another way to use garbage cans is to attach them to caster-mounted dollies. This works particularly well if the storage center has a concrete floor.

• *Pull-out bins* can be sized to fit available space, but the most convenient spot for them is under a workbench. Here, the bins can be used in place or pulled out when they are nearly empty.

Poisons, sprayers, and valuables should be kept in a locked cabinet. A locked cabinet is a must for anyone who uses chemicals for pest and disease control, especially when there are small children around. Inexpensive wood or metal boxes can be bolted to a wall out of a child's reach. It is best to keep these storage boxes in the garage or some other sheltered place outside the house.

Barbecuing equipment needs protection from rain, fog, and snow. Fabric covers can blow off; equipment will be better preserved during winter in a storage shed. Barbecuing accessories also must be kept dry; try storing charcoal briquettes in metal or plastic cans with tight lids so they won't absorb moisture.

Screens and storm sashes can be kept on ceiling racks. Build the racks with bolts if they're for storm windows; screen racks can be built with nails. Offset every other sash an inch or two; the hardware prevents them from being stacked flat.

Boats and boating gear sometimes fall under zoning restrictions—some areas prohibit parking boats, with or without trailers, on residential property. Boats need a protected place; heavy canvas covers are only partial protection. If you have a small boat, try standing it upright and tying it to a wall with rope. Larger boats can be hung horizontally on a wall, bottom out, with support on both sides.

An even better method is bottom down with a padded cradle supporting the hull at several points. Hoist the cradle on pulleys secured to joists. The amount of weight the cradle will bear depends on the size of the boat and the strength of the garage or shed structure. To hold more weight, suspend the boat from more than just two or three joists and hang pulleys near top edges of the joists.

Lightweight gear can be stored inside the boat or hung on a wall. Store outboard motors and sails in a dry place.

Bicycles stored for a long period of time should be hung from a ceiling joist on ropes or hooks or hung from a wall on long brackets or hooks. If the tires rest on the floor for an extended time, they'll flatten and crack as air gradually escapes.

Bike parking problem?

Brightly colored hooks support bikes by one wheel for repairs, by both wheels when cars kept in garage.

T-shaped rack for two bikes hangs from garage roof joist. Adjust rack dimensions according to size of your bikes, garage height, height of car underneath.

Brackets screwed into wall secure bikes; weight rests on rear wheels. Nail goes through holes on both sides of bracket and between bike's spokes to lock wheel in place. Brackets could be made of metal, wood, or plastic.

Storing boats & heavy gear

Hinged brace holds rack away from house, unhooks (at bottom right) to fold rack flat. Boat ties to pairs of rope eyes; carpeting scraps protect finish.

Three-purpose sail locker hinges sideways to open, holds sails, booms, lines convenient to dock. Both ends of top hinge up to make chaise lounge. Or use locker-bench to store garden umbrellas, barbecue equipment on a patio. Locker requires no bottom when resting on a planked wood deck; air circulates up through decking to dry wet sails. If placed over concrete, locker needs raised wood bottom with ventilation holes.

Two loops of rope, one around bow and one for stern, run through pulleys attached to overhead rafter. Car fits underneath suspended boat.

Four doors of shed open wide – anything, everything becomes accessible. Raised floor helps keep shed dry, has ramp for wheelbarrow, lawnmower. Potting counter includes three bins below for peat moss and mulches. Bin front hinges down for easy access; two outer drawers tilt downward when pulled out; notched board, with pieces of plastic garden hose nailed to edge, stores long-handled tools upright.

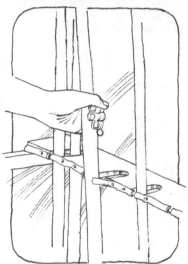

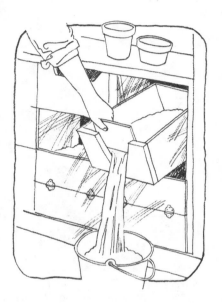

Two garden work centers

Potting and storage bench includes leaf drop, two bins for potting mixtures, retractable hose, sink. Designer: Gene Dunn.

Garden tools are ready to use

Coiled hose fits *between studs in a metal-lined opening cut in an exterior wall; four nails hold hose in place. Designers: Don and Fil Drukey.*

Tool rack *made from a hotel pot hanger attaches high on garage wall, keeps floor clear. Screw eyes in ends of handles slip over hooks.*

Bench has room inside *for a long hose and a faucet. Sheet of galvanized tin set underneath deters termites. Designers: Don and Fil Drukey.*

Storage for pads, cushions

Bar on upper rack, *attached to studs with lag bolt and washer, raises to slip pad into place.*

Wrought iron rod *attached to house wall on covered porch takes up little space, allows air circulation.*

A built-in barbecuing center

Outdoor kitchen's two upper doors become counters when dropped down on chains held by screw eyes, unhook for more walk-by space. Vertical door on end conceals long tools; top serves as plant display counter.

Garage storage miscellany

Window shades make inexpensive doors for a cabinet, roll out of way without wasting space.

Above-car loft made of wide, sturdy shelving supports bulk storage, would fit in a garage or workshop. Designer: George Peters.

Hammock hung just under garage ceiling serves as convenient catchall for often-used sports equipment and conforms to awkward shapes.

Underneath garden work counter, *bulky nursery sacks fit to left of vertical post. To right, low shelf separates stacks of clay pots. Carport roof shelters supplies. Architects: Robert C. Peterson, Victor K. Thompson.*

Using your carport for storage

Anchored *between two posts of carport, storage bin holds garden pots, bicycles. Architects: Terry and Moore.*

Divider between carport *and entry walk has shelves for suitcases, trunks, and car washing equipment. Tools hang on back wall panel. Designer: Neil Crawford.*

Each tool has its place and its special hanger on long wooden panel above workbench. Two lipped shelves for cans of paint and cans filled with small parts keep all supplies visible. (See page 84.)

The right tool in the right place

Rolling workbench takes big projects, clutter outside.

Assorted jars for nails and other small parts screw or pop off the lids nailed underneath workshop shelves.

Rolling box holds usable scraps, kindling, fits into corner. Top has two hinges.

Vertical cabinets store long garden implements; chemicals on top shelf.

Bright canvas awning conceals paint, lumber, tools on shallow shelves next to garage door.

Index

Photographers